NORTHWEST TERRITORIES

45.

44.

35.

22.

ALBERTA

SASKATCHEWAN

MANITOBA

10.

20.
19.

21.

33.
32.
34.

24.
23.
25.

18.
17.

41.

28.
31.   26.
27.

7.
8.

4.
3.   6.

39.

15.
14.
16.

5.

2.

38.

29.   30.

9.

1.

12.
11.   13.

N

OVER THE COUNTER

The Country Store in Canada

by
ENID MALLORY

Fitzhenry & Whiteside

© 1985 Enid Mallory

Fitzhenry & Whiteside Limited
195 Allstate Parkway
Markham, Ontario L3R 4T8

Editors   Peter Taylor
            Patrick Crean
            Frank English
Design   Word & Image
Endpaper maps   David Prothero
Typesetting   Jay Tee Graphics Ltd.

Printed and bound in Canada by T. H. Best Printing Company

Canadian Cataloguing in Publication Data
Mallory, Enid L.
   Over the counter: the country store in Canada
ISBN 0-88902-989-X
1. General stores - Canada. I. Title.
HF5429.6.C3M34   381′.1′0971   C85-099192-7

CONTENTS

For Mildred and Milton Swerdfeger
in memory

for Joyce Swerdfeger Judd
and Lillian Christie Henderson,
and for all the Glen Stewart customers

Photograph Credits

ACKNOWLEDGEMENTS

Stories written down by my father when he was 79, got this book started. A grant from the Ontario Arts Council widened its scope.

What kept it going across a very big country, was the momentum of enthusiasm from the storytellers. To these I am deeply indebted for sharing the high moments of their lives . . . the laughs, the bad times, the deep satisfaction, and the strong conviction that this was a marvelous country to live in. Store-keeping, (so most of you said) was a work-all-day-and-night-but-miss-it-terribly-when-you-quit kind of job.

The namcs of storekeepers and customers who shared their stories are at the end of each story. Their addresses are where the story took place rather than where they live now, when these are not the same. In a few cases, the names within the stories have been changed, or the names of contributors omitted to protect the "innocent".

I am indebted to other people who were not the storytellers but who helped me find them, or who searched out the history of a particular store. I will try to name most of them: Lloyd MacLeod, Vernon River, P.E.I.; Hal Higgins, Sydney, N.S.; Hank and Carley Martin, Rothesay, N.B.; Mr. and Mrs. Aiton, Hartland, N.B.; Jocelyn Choquette, Compton, Que.; in Ontario, Ross and Edith Anderson, Prescott; Eva and Jimmy McMillan, Martintown; Joyce and Ross Judd, Dundas; Wilfred and Del Hansen, Timmins; Barbara Sauder, Indian River; Helen Wilcox, Bridgenorth; Arlene Stephens, Bruce Struthers, Doris Tarasuk, Gail Corbett, Merle Collins, Eleanor Swerdfeger, Elwood Jones, Mary Harrison, all of Peterborough; Mary Dziadow, Arborg, Man.; Howard and Barbara Jamieson, Winnipeg, Man.; John Struthers, Saskatoon, Sask.; Muriel Stillborn, Duff, Sask.; Jessie Campbell, Castor, Alta.; Gertrude Tackacs, Pavilion, B.C.

Arlene Stephens and Gord Mallory were my editor-advisors in the book's early stage. Peter Taylor, Patrick Crean and Frank English were my editors at Fitzhenry & Whiteside.

A special thanks to Gord, Jonathan, Allison and Laurie who went to the far corners of Canada with me, and to Peter who stayed home and worked.

One of the many moods of the country store is caught in this photo taken in the Menie store at Century Village, Lang near Peterborough, Ontario. Milton Swerdfeger and Gord Mallory play an impromptu game of checkers by the stove.

INTRODUCTION

To grow up in a country store is to be at the centre of a very small universe. At the core of our universe in Glen Stewart, Ontario was a big pot-bellied stove radiating warmth like a sun. Around it circled the customers, stopping to open the stove door and spit tobacco juice, like pagans in some ancient rite of worship to their sun.

There are sounds that linger forever for anyone who has spent time in a country store: the jingle of the bell when the door opened, blizzards that howled around the front stoop, horses and sleigh bells in the early days, laughter and the jumble of voices on a Saturday night, a child tapping his coin on the candy showcase, the squeaking of the hanging British American Gasoline sign when the wind blew outside.

Smells too: brown sugar when you opened the bin, plug tobacco under the counter, spices weighed on the scales near Christmas time, farmers in coonskin coats on a wet day, pungent pipes smoked beside the stove, pig-starter, bran and shorts and middlings, in the feedshed.

But it was probably the stories told beside the pot-bellied stove that made me set out in 1982 to record what has happened in the country stores of Canada. Old timers in the Glen Stewart store tipped back their chairs and pushed memory back until you were there with the pioneers digging the Iroquois Canal or putting the first bridge across Sandy Creek. Younger men talked about the war they had just come through, and extended the Glen Stewart universe to the outer space of Normandy and North Africa. Then someone stomped in and said Aunt May had pneumonia. Conversation shifted back and forth from local to worldwide events. The country store was a capsule of everyday life as it happened.

At least some of this rich legacy could be captured on a tape recorder and written down. When I set out to do it from coast to coast, Canada looked like a very big country. For no particular reason I headed west first. When I told rancher Howard Humphrey, at Knutsford, British Columbia, what I was doing, he exclaimed, "All of Canada!"; then added with the dry humour typical of Westerners, "Oh my gosh, you'll be two weeks!"

A year later I sat in a grand old house in Twillingate, Newfoundland talking to two storekeepers whose lives were intimately linked with the sea. I thought of the 7000-odd kilometres that stretch between the storekeepers of Twillingate and those of British Columbia's dry grasslands and coastal mountains. Yet I could hear the same overtones in what they were saying, the same *joie de vivre*, the conviction that theirs was a wonderful life: "Tell your readers that this is God's country and we've been spared to see the best of both worlds." Then, whether I sat in Newfoundland or Quebec or Saskatchewan or British Columbia, they would proceed to tell me about the hardships of their early days with as much delight as when they described their successes of later years. The conclusion I soon reached is that country storekeepers loved a challenge. And, right across the country, they got just that.

Most of them came through a depression and the stresses and strains of one or two world wars, while they dealt head-on with fires, floods, drought, bad debts, robberies, runaway horses and whatever other disasters came their way.

These people and the lives they lived are now etched on my mind. Because I have met them, I find myself at odd moments wondering what someone on the southern tip of Nova Scotia is doing, or whether there is snow yet at Lilooet on British Columbia's Fraser River. Portraits pop into my head at odd times: Bill McNeil sitting on the veranda of his store by the Toqique River in New Brunswick, caught in the horizontal light of a setting sun; Myrs Tretiak, veteran storekeeper-farmer, out picking stones in his northern Manitoba field, as he was on the day I interviewed him there; Katie MacLeod among her flowers, young and vibrant at ninety-two, and still in love with her Prince Edward Island store; Fred Frederickson of Glenboro, Manitoba at ninety-three, saying, "I wouldn't miss my life for anything . . . from 1889 'til now, 1982."

There are places I remember vividly: an Alberta farmhouse near Coronation on an August night. As a group of us sat around the kitchen table, a thunderstorm was roaring outside. As ninety-four-year-old Jack Hallett, who was there before the railway, delivered the punch line of his best story, lightning struck, the lights went out and the tape recorder went off, and we sat there in total darkness and laughed.

I remember another kitchen in Rocky Harbour, Newfoundland where I shared a delicious meal of corn cod and home-made bread with the young man who cooked it and the old man who told me stories going back to the turn of the century.

I remember a parking lot at Dauphin, Manitoba where I interviewed Olga and Alec Petreshan after we had watched the annual Ukrainian Festival Parade.

I remember miles and miles of lonely roads as we drove to Cape Negro on the south coast of Nova Scotia. Then suddenly there were cars and cars and cars, all lined along the crossroads where a ball game was underway. For a while we had been like city visitors thinking the land was empty. But there it was, all the lively energy of rural Canada which could be focused wherever there was a ball game or a church social or a country store.

As early as 1860 there were an estimated 4000 country stores across Canada; and now, 125 years later, we have about the same number. What happened in between is the real story. Country stores established themselves in towns and villages and outports wherever farmers or fishermen or lumbermen lived, on mountains, in valleys, where rivers met, where roads crossed, where bridges were built, where railways ran, or logging roads, by fur trappers' trails, where gold was found. By 1930, Statistics Canada reported that there were 11 915 country stores. In 1941, they peaked at 11 917.

The typical country store of 1941 had counters on each side and shelves along the walls, holding groceries, tobacco, dry goods, wallpaper, harness, paint, hardware, boots and shoes, glass and dishes, patent medicines and veterinary supplies. Gas pumps stood beside the store. Usually a storehouse and feed-shed were attached to the store; often a small barn or shed stood some distance from the store. "Out" buildings would contain flour and feed, seed grain, coal oil, shingles, fencing, cement, coal . . . and even pigs, cows and chickens.

In the last forty years, in heavily populated parts of Canada, as country stores, along with mills and cheese factories and blacksmith shops, began to disappear, some communities have reconstructed pioneer villages which feature authentic country stores. In Compton, Quebec, a very special Parks Canada restoration is the childhood home and store of Prime Minister Louis St. Laurent. In such places, visitors can lean on the old counters and catch some of the flavour of old stores.

Even better than restored stores, are the "survivors", the ones that have never been closed and never been modernized. In every province, there are places where time has "gone easy" with the country store and let it ripen like vintage wine. The old benches are still there, the bell still dangles over the door to ring as you come in. The bins are still there, or the Diamond Dye cabinets, the wooden counters, sometimes the balance scales or an ornate cash register, sometimes the old stove.

I found "survivor" stores in every part of Canada, places where someone who grew up in a 1940 store could feel at home, where the look and the sounds and the smells are right. Bill McNeil, when asked to remember the Cape Breton stores of his youth, said, "Every store had a smell of its own, but the overriding smell would be dried fish . . . stacks of great big cod-fish two or three feet high."

For me, from smalltown Ontario, the smells are of harness leather and wood smoke and puffed wheat and rubber boots and coal oil and spices. The exact flavour varies as we move north, south, east and west. This book will wander across Canada to bring back the sounds and sights and smells and moods and memories associated with the country stores that ar gone – and make us treasure the 4000-odd stores we have left.

CHAPTER ONE

WHERE THE ACTION WAS

Country stores may be quiet places today . . . sometimes they are bread-and-milk stops where people run in and pass the time of day for only a moment or two. But two generations ago, they were where it all happened. You went there for the action, the gossip, the laughs, the fun, the highjinks.

Lady Sarah (McCrea) Eaton, born in Omemee, Ontario, before the turn of the century, wrote of growing up there when her uncle, Isaac McNeilly, kept the general store: "Omemee seemed to me a wonderful place, full of interesting people and exciting things to do at all seasons of the year."

In the first part of this century, small towns were still young, particularly in the West where everyone had come from somewhere else, and you could homestead at 18. A sense of adventure might have brought you here, but it made a strange bedfellow with the loneliness, endless work and sometimes boredom of your 160 acres. Out on the prairies there was a distinct lack of people, but along the tracks of the Canadian Pacific Railway and the Canadian National Railways, in towns like Moosomin and Maple Creek and Wainwright, you could find people, tell stories and make some fun.

In all parts of Canada, country stores were favourite settings for practical jokes. In every community there was someone who was different, a foreigner, a hermit, or someone who belonged to an odd religion, or there was a good friend who "had one up on you". As Mr. Bennet said in Pride and Prejudice, "For what do we live, but to make sport of our neighbours, and laugh at them in our turn."

Every community has its honour roll of colourful characters who frequented the country store. Much of the action centred around them. They were laughed at, loved, sometimes hated, and talked about for 40 years after.

Mostly the action was happy, sometimes it wasn't: jolly reunions as a traveller came home to the village; the shock of someone's sudden death; fights outside the store; runaway horses; romances on the store veranda; robberies; crazy pranks.

If you were there, you saw it happen.

Horses, pigs, dogs and people, they were all there at the Campbellton store (midway between London and Chatham, Ontario) when the photographer came.

WITH MY AIRFORCE KNIFE

*T*here used to be a lot of people who would drink anything. This man came in bound to have pure vanilla. I said, "We don't have it."

He said, "You do so have it. Your husband would sell it to me if he was here."

"That's what you think."

"Well, there's some right up there." He pointed at little bottles of food colouring.

"That is for icing, it's oily stuff." I set one down on the counter to show him. When I turned my back for a minute, he up and drank it. I said, "Now you drank it, you pay for it!"

"No sir!" He wasn't going to pay for anything.

We had a big airforce knife with a fifteen-inch blade and four-inch rosewood handle. We always kept it between the paper rack and the cash register. I grabbed that knife and I came around the end of the counter and I said, "Now you get out and don't ever let me catch you in here again." I chased him right to the door.

There was another fellow who had been with him and he was coming in to see what was holding up his friend, but when he saw me coming with the knife, he took off down the road.

Mae Melville,
Stickney, New Brunswick

BIGOTRY AND BULLETS

*T*he pounding on the store door started in the middle of the night. The man was yelling that his partner was hurt . . . shot. Our building had one of those upstairs "suicide doors" that eastern Ontario houses often have; Dad had built a porch around it. Before Mother would let Dad go down there, she went out on this porch and yelled down, "Why? What were you doing? People don't get shot around here for doing nothing."

The man yelled back that they were Jehovah's Witnesses. That changed the picture; there were people in the area that had no use for the Jehovah's Witness sect. So Mother and Dad went down to help and brought them into the store. They phoned the police and the doctor, nine miles away in Iroquois. I remember how angry my mother was that the doctor and the policeman stopped for coffee before coming; the man was suffering.

I also remember being hurried out of the store and over to the Tousants' house, so that we missed most of what went on. But afterward, the discussion and the controversy in the store went on for a long time. The two men had been camped in the schoolyard in a van. A neighbour, who was caretaker of the school, ordered them out. Before they could go, he started shooting. He hit a tire first, then hit the driver in the arm. That man would lose the use of that arm for the rest of his life.

Neighbours of the man who did the shooting got together as witnesses. When his day came in court, they got him off. But other neighbours were deeply shocked, my parents among them. Their sympathy was with the man who got shot.

Enid Swerdfeger,
Glen Stewart, Ontario

COMING UP TO CHRISTMAS

*T*he best time was coming up to Christmas when the pails of candy and simple gifts came in. They weren't opened until the day we hung up the tissue-paper bells and streamers . . . and unpacked the pails of bullseyes, creams, chocolates, candy brooms, licorice and lozenges with sayings on them . . . and the toiletries, fancy gloves, stockings and stuff that people bought for presents.

The store was always crowded on Christmas eve. Men buying things on the sly. Women consulting my mother to buy ties, shirts, etc. for husbands. And then at 11:30, the Catholics would start to drift across the street for Midnight Mass and the Protestants would go home . . . and at midnight the store closed and we went to Mass . . . and the place was warm, smelling of cedar boughs and brilliant with candles and gas lamps and the choir would start to sing the carols and hymns . . . and there was a warm, comfortable feeling of peace on earth . . . and we felt protected and at ease . . . .

Harry J. Boyle,
St. Augustine, Ontario

*Some sense of the action that stirred
around a store in a mining town, is
conveyed in this posed photo taken
in Cobalt, Ontario, where silver
was discovered in 1903.*

GLUTEN JUICE

*T*he best stories which Dad would tell in the truck on the way home from Cardinal were about earlier days when the Canada Starch Company had a by-product for which the company had no use. Every so often they would announce that this gluten juice, or "swill" as the farmers called it, was available *free*.

Such news spread like wildfire. It was eighteen miles from Glen Stewart to Cardinal, but gluten swill made grand pig feed. At midnight before the appointed day, our customers would hitch their teams, put every available container on their wagons and race each other to Cardinal.

Long before dawn, the teams would be in line for the precious swill that would whet the appetites of their pigs. While a few sober men remained to watch the teams, the pigs' masters would be whetting their own appetites and quenching their thirsts in the Cardinal hotel.

With a touch of local pride in his voice, Dad told the story of William Ellis and Little Johnny Gilmer and the night they got into a fight with a roomful of Cardinal farmers. Ellis was a big man, Gilmer as robust and wiry as he was little. These two actually cleaned out the room, throwing a number of Cardinal men through the window of the hotel.

In the morning, drunk or sober, the men would race their teams to the swill vats the minute the gates swung open. Buckets would dip into the vats and splash swill into wagon containers in a scene of chaos. Such was the excitement of something free that some of the men would jump into the vats, scoop up the pails of swill and pass them out to a partner filling the wagon containers.

Then wet, ridiculous, well satisfied, and just a little bit sheepishly, they would go home to the disapproval of their wives and the delight of their pigs.

Enid Swerdfeger,
Glen Stewart, Ontario

OVER THE BARREL HEAD FIRST

*L*ots of funny things happened in Champion. At that time local option was voted in, you see, so you couldn't have liquor around. And the men who built the hotel were quite a hand for drinking booze. And when this local option first came in, they shipped out several barrels to their farm east of town.

Finally one day a barrel of whiskey came in with no bill of lading, and was settin' on the livery platform over there. And nobody went near it. It was against the law to buy it. Or sell it. And we had two Mounties stationed here in town. We were watching the Mounties and they were watching that barrel. One of them goes out every morning and gives the barrel a boost to see how heavy it is . . . that none has been taken out of it.

It had set there about three weeks and they were watching it. Every morning they'd test it. So this morning in particular we was watching her, and the Mountie gives a real heave on her and goes over the barrel head first. There wasn't a drop in it. Not a drop in it.

He got up rubbing his shins, and came through town looking around and came to the store. Of course, nobody knew anything about it, you know.

Whoever did it, they drilled a hole about that big around right up through the bottom . . . they got underneath the platform there and drilled right on up through the platform . . . and they drained it!

Harvey Beaubier,
Champion, Alberta

UNDER THE LILAC TREE

*I*n the 1950s, the building of the St. Lawrence Seaway changed life at Glen Stewart. Farmers who had rarely seen ready cash could now get good-paying jobs on the Seaway project. At 7:30 in the mornings, Seaway workers stopped by the store for gasoline or cigarettes or work gloves. On Friday nights most of them stopped to cash cheques and buy groceries. One Friday night the Glen Stewart store had nine men in line to cash cheques as in a bank. Dad once took 41 cheques to the bank in Iroquois. "And I had a long name to sign 41 times," he remembers.

One day in 1958, a car stopped beside the store and Dad saw two men sit and look the store over. Then they drove south two miles to the Hainsville store where they robbed J.P. Murray and fired a shot through the ceiling, narrowly missing a woman and child who sat in a rocking chair in their living quarters above the store.

After that Father and Mother began to bury money under the lilac tree. Dad dug a hole into which he slipped a glass sealer containing the extra money from the till each night.

I should add . . . in case anyone is tempted to dig behind the present-day Glen Stewart store some dark night . . . that they were careful not to leave any money under the lilac tree when they moved away in 1959.

Enid Swerdfeger,
Glen Stewart, Ontario

WE HAD A STAMPEDE

*W*e kept a complete line in our store at Rocky Mountain House . . . horseshoe nails, harness, warm clothing, men's underwear. As the town grew and more stores started up in the early sixties, I could see what way things were going and I decided I'd be better to go to just groceries. So I got up one morning and told the staff I was going to clear out all dry goods. I put a small sign in the window which said ALL DRY GOODS, HALF PRICE.

We had a stampede. That day we took in $4000. I had to hire untrained people and post a guard at the front door and the back . . . goods were disappearing out the back. People lined up and we would let them in 10 to 15 at a time, and lock the door. People came from as far away as Eckville.

In the back room of the store, that was the warehouse, we had taken in a shipment of sweaters and they were all on the shelves, all stacked nicely in the cartons. And the women would read the labels and pick out the size they wanted and pull it out, and if it suited them they'd put it under their arms and come and pay for it. But if it didn't suit them, a lot of them would just drop it on the floor, and we had all kinds of sweaters and boxes that people were tramping all over. They went wild.

This went on for about a week, and within a week we cleared all the extraneous goods out . . . right down to the needles and threads. I'll tell you, out in the back shed we had things up on rafters and people would even get up on the rafters. And we had a refrigerator plant for meat, and one woman got up on the refrigerator and she couldn't get down. We had to help her down.

Joe and Jenny Cony,
Rocky Mountain House, Alberta

JACK ADAMS

*A*cross the road from our Glen Stewart store was a blacksmith shop run by Jack Adams, "an unconcerned worker". Sometimes when a farmer came to get work done, Jack could not be found.

But if you could find Jack, no one could shoe a horse any better. No matter how ugly or mean the horse. I watched him shoe one that was a vicious kicker. He managed to get a rope on one hind foot and stretch that leg out so the horse could not kick. After he shod that foot, he got a rope on the other hind leg and did the same with it.

Jack liked his drink. He owed me a grocery bill. When he came home drunk, it might mean he had some money, so I would hurry over to his house to collect on his bill, and Jack would cheerfully give me what he had.

But if you "got one up" on Jack, he would be watching for a chance to put the laugh on you. I needed the loan of a horse to drive 15 miles to Spencerville to meet my wife, Mildred, coming home by train from Ottawa. Jack gave me a horse that was an outlaw. Although I had handled horses all my life, I found this one uncontrollable. When I reached the highway at Spencerville, the horse put on its best effort and took me tearing through the village while Mildred stood on the station platform watching what she thought was some stranger's runaway horse. When I got the "outlaw" stopped and came back to the station, she had to face the terrifying truth that this horse would be taking her home. When we reached home safely . . . in record time . . . Jack had a fine laugh, said he had never driven the beast himself.

Jack did a lot of horse-trading, and always got the best of the deal. If he had a deal in the offing or if someone wanted a horse shod, he told them always to call to our store . . . collect. We never accepted Jack's collect calls, but he enjoyed trying it.

If the calls were not collect, Mildred would go to the front store door and "Yoo Hoo" at Jack. On the first of April she had been fooled by Jack early in the day. Now, the flood was up all around Jack's house, so in the afternoon she faked a long distance call and "Yoo Hoo'd" urgently to Jack. Phones were still regarded with respect in those days; long distance calls had a kind of awe about them. Jack rose to her bait; instead of going a long way around to stay dry, he came splashing through the water, soaking himself. She let him say hello a few times before she "April Fooled" him.

Another time, to get even for one of Jack's jokes, we changed clothing, Mildred in a man's clothing and me in a dress. We went over to where Jack was working in his shop and asked if he knew where the Swerdfegers were. He didn't know, and he had no idea who he was talking to. We visited a while, then left. Next day we told Jack who the two strangers were.

Milton Swerdfeger,
Glen Stewart, Ontario

GRAVEYARD HIGH JINKS

Pony Moore and Vince McCarthy were in the Victoria House Hotel across from the graveyard and kitty-corner across from the store. Someone said they'd buy drinks for the house if these two would walk through the graveyard and back. So they walked over the hill down toward the far fence.

Mick Keaneally had a lamp and he could move it so it would light this one particular tombstone so you'd swear there was a light right over that grave. John B. Doris and Dennis Roach had sneaked out and they'd stole two of Aunt Mary's white sheets and draped themselves, and there was a fresh grave dug so they got down behind the mound of dirt. Just as Pony and Vince, on the way back, got opposite them, they raised up and started to groan. Pony and Vince saw the light and the white figures and they took off and hit the wire fence at the end of the graveyard like a herd of buffalo.

Of course people at the hotel and the store were out watching it happen . . . this was the whole deal.

Phil Beattie,
Keene, Ontario

PUTTING PETER SMYTHE IN HIS PLACE

Peter Smythe died in 1878, so no one living here in Port Hood now ever actually knew him. But, when we first came here, we stayed in Mrs. MacDonald's tourist home. Her mother was a little old lady who sat in a corner and said nothing. But we got to talking, telling the tales about Peter Smythe's store and wishing someone had actually known him, and suddenly she said, "I saw Peter Smythe once."

"I was a little girl about five and I remember being in his store one day. He was a big, important man by this time, had been a Member of Parliament for quite a while. A country woman was in the store with a sack of potatoes to barter and she was not getting waited on. Finally she said, 'Peter Smythe, are you going to wait on me or not?'

"Peter gave her a look of scorn, 'I'll have you know my name has a proper handle on it.'

"The woman's answer came without hesitation, 'So does a piss pot!' "

Paul McCulloch,
Port Hood, Nova Scotia

EIGHT JOBS AT ONCE

I had eight different jobs. We built the store in Old Chelsea and we ran the store. We were asked to cater for Camp Fortune Ski Hill which was two lodges then, and we built it up to five. Fourteen thousand people! I fed all those people. And I had six children. We ran school buses. And we had Crown Studio's cafeteria on Scott Road; that was where they did the RCMP series *Inside Out*. I got on Council, first woman councillor in western Quebec. Then we bought this old building at Farm Point, which was a vegetable stand, and we built the store there, the Lagacé Mini Market. And we used to deliver groceries to Kingsmere, Tenaga, Gleneagle, Larrimac, Burnet. I delivered after I closed the store at night. My brother and husband did this too, but after my first husband died, I did it. Close the store at 11 o'clock at night, then deliver. I can remember going up to Kingsmere when the rut was a foot deep and I couldn't get out of it. If a car had been coming down, I couldn't turn out.

I got all this done by sleeping three hours a night. I would come in that door from Camp Fortune and sit there to take off my boots and I'd fall asleep with my head on the table. It might be 12 o'clock, and at two or three o'clock in the morning I'd wake up. We had Camp Fortune for 14 years and the store 28 years.

We lived behind the store. The kids were tied outside with harness to the trees, with a big pile of sand in the summertime. Lots of times I was alone in the store and couldn't watch them. My husband would be gone with a bus or gone to town for groceries, or to the packing house.

The CBC came here in 1965 to do a show which they called *Living With Mrs. Irene Boland.* They followed me from 7:45 in the morning until six o'clock at night and they were played out. I said, "You're played out, but I have to keep going until 12."

The way it was, there was no money and you had to do it. I said to my first husband (I didn't think he was going to die), "When we are 60 years old we won't have to work any more. We will have enough saved." We had insurance policies and it was hard to pay them, really hard. That's why I drove the school bus.

And I sold Avon! Oh! This lady came and wanted me to take it. She said, "You have so many places that you deliver orders anyway, where you could sell Avon too." You know, I was their best representative in this area. I sent in $500- and $600-orders every three weeks.

What did I enjoy? I didn't enjoy any of it. It was too much work! Oh, I loved the people though. I knew everybody. You can get used to very little sleep.

And having my babies, oh I still worked then! After Chris was born, I got out of bed to put a fire in the Quebec heater. He was born about 10:30 at night and I got up about one o'clock to put the fire on. My husband was so tired that once he fell asleep, I couldn't wake him up.

Now that we're retired, I never find it too quiet. No way! It's secluded here in Old Chelsea. I don't even want the radio on. I just love that feeling of quietness floating right in, like as if you were near the water.

Irene (Boland) Lagacé,
Old Chelsea, Quebec

CHAPTER TWO

EARLY DAYS

Often the person behind the counter had no experience whatever at keeping store, and hardly any money in his pocket . . . but he could do it. What he needed was flexibility, the ability to bargain and barter, a willingness to try anything, at least a thousand practical skills, the strength to work from dawn to dusk, endless patience, a love of people and a great sense of humour.

With all these qualifications, he still needed luck. His luck followed the luck of his customers. If the market in hogs or lumber or wheat bottomed out, his business did too. If drought or hail or grasshoppers destroyed the prairie farmers' crops, the store by the CPR tracks would be desperate too. If the fishery off Prince Edward Island or Newfoundland was bad, the storekeepers were in the same boat as the fishermen. Without his customers, a storekeeper was nothing.

Where the community was new, the building was not very important at first. If the customers were there, the storekeeper could sell from a packing crate. A tent would do nicely. Labour was cheap in those early days, and a person could get a log building up in short order. More than one Western store was built from packing crates in a place and time where lumber was scarce and the money to buy it even scarcer.

Getting those first goods to the store was sometimes difficult. If you came by railway, you brought the goods with you. In the older parts of Canada, in the days before railways, merchants moved the goods by water or carted them over rough bush trails that could mix tea and sugar and salt all together, and reduce crockery to little pieces.

But the possibilities were endless if the seller were versatile. He could grind the farmers' grain. He could pull teeth and cut hair. He could butcher hogs and cattle and sell the meat. He could deal in eggs and butter and potash and seneca roots and muskrat hides. He could sell sugar and flour, tobacco and calico and blocks of blue salt, harness and dishes and silk stockings, woollen underwear and Rundle's Liniment, men's suits and Dogskin or Wombat coats.

And looking back, those were the best days of all. He was young. The world was young. He was starting out to become a great entrepreneur.

And sometimes he did just that!

This attractive pine clapboard store at Doon Pioneer Village near Kitchener, Ontario is a replica of the Delaware store, west of London, dated from 1835. Inside are molds for maple sugar, woodframe skates, wolf traps, horse collars and cattle leaders, stone crockery, bonnets and underwear, spices and candy and patent medicines, tobacco cutters and a cheese cutter and a stove that dates back to the 1880s.

THE PACKING BOX WAS HIS COUNTER

My grandfather, Klaas Reimer, came here to Manitoba as a Mennonite immigrant in 1874. They came as farmers, settled in the wilderness. He really started the store incidentally. They went to Winnipeg for their trade, there was a trail to there . . . Indian trails were the only roads then . . . and they began to build bridges over swamps. In 1877, they went to Winnipeg for supplies . . . two or three of them together. R.J. Whitla, the manager there, offered to let him take home a supply so that he could serve the customers out there. He said, "I have no money." Mr. Whitla said, "You don't need to have any money. You sell that at home and then you bring me the money after that."

He took dry goods, clothing, a boxful home . . . $300 worth. When he got home and unpacked it, he turned the wooden packing box upside down and that was his counter. And he was in business.

They lived in sod houses at first. They had come from the Ukraine; there the sod was solid, but here it was kind of loose and when it rained outside they soon noticed it on the floor. As soon as they could, they built a log house. A little later, he built a frame house and he used the old log house as a store. Later on, he built an addition to the store.

He had sons and the sons helped him, and they took hides, vegetables. And that's how the trade went on. And then he took his sons into partnership as the business began to grow. In 1866, one of his sons, Henry H.W. Reimer, started a hardware

In the early 1900s, the Reimer store in Steinbach, Manitoba grew to an enormous size. It had 14 full-time employees and "took in trade all farm products from seneca roots to horse hair".

store at an angle across the street from his father's store. In the
end that was a general store too.

John C. Reimer,
Steinbach, Manitoba

WE'LL HAUL IT FOR YOU

I grew up in New London (Prince Edward Island) and we came
down here in 1923. I thought it would be fun to have a store.
We drove around and we came to Vernon River. We noticed
the big church and the three mills. It looked like a real good
location.

So we moved into a house where the owner had had a Rawleigh route (sold door to door), and he had a room upstairs fixed
up with shelves. We moved in September, and my husband
took over the Rawleigh route to get acquainted with the people
around here. As he went around, he told them he was going to
start a store.

Well, November first was a Holy Day in the Catholic
church and the word had got around that a store was opening
in our house. Grandma and I were alone . . . my husband was
out on his route . . . and we looked out and there were so many
sleighs! One man came in and said, "We hear you are starting a
store."

"Well," I said, "our shipment from Carvells and DeBloise's
is at the station. It just came and we haven't got it yet."

"Well," he said, "I want twist tobacco. We've got sleighs
here and we'll haul all that order down for you."

So away they went. I remember they brought back a
35-gallon tierce of molasses, hauled it down and put it in a
garage that we had, and put a spiggot in it. There was sugar and
an 11-pound caddy of twist tobacco . . . 10¢ a twist, Hickey &
Nicholson tobacco.

So when my husband came home and heard what had
happened, he said, "Well, I guess I won't go out on the road
anymore." And we had our store.

Katie MacLeod,
Vernon River, Prince Edward Island

INSTEAD OF TEETH

This is John Crysler's store, at Upper Canada Village in Ontario, as it looked in the early 1820s.

This store was started in 1873. Mrs. John Fummerton. Her father gave her $20 to buy teeth. She went to Perth and used the $20 to buy groceries instead and started the Fallbrook store.

Walter Cameron,
Fallbrook, Ontario

GENTLEMEN OF GOOD COURAGE WANTED

I was born in Dundee, Scotland, July 4th, 1906, and as a reader of Ballantyne, Henty and the exploits of Mallory, Franklin, Scott, etc., I was anxious to venture into foreign lands for a more adventurous life.

This wish was granted when my mother pointed out to me an add in the Edinburgh *Scotsman*, a newspaper we bought only occasionally, which read, "Wanted: young men of good courage with the spirit of adventure for northern fur trade posts in Canada. Apply etc."

I applied and was accepted along with 32 other young men in that year of 1927. In June, we sailed for Canada in the one-year-old Hudson's Bay ship, the *S.S. Bayrupert*, out of Ardrossan. Seven sea-sick days later, we pulled into Montreal and there we were split up with groups posted to the Arctic, Quebec, Ontario, Manitoba and other western parts. I was slated for Cumberland House, Saskatchewan.

To get to Cumberland House I had to go by rail to Winnipeg, then on to The Pas and there was given a choice of paddle steamer or canoe with two Indians. Being "of good courage etc.", I and another clerk chose the Indians and set off across, I think, Saskeram Lake, which is farmland today, then on to the Saskatchewan River. We were two nights on the trip and the mosquitoes were something new for us, but we had mosquito nets so we slept o.k.

Cumberland House was an old historic post. The store had two long counters, which provided sitting room for the Indians who spent all day with us, and behind the counters was the shelving filled with groceries, yard goods, ammunition, etc. Assorted hardware, such as pails and kettles, was suspended from the ceiling. The staples were lard, flour, baking powder, tobacco, tea and sugar. The lard came in huge barrels and had to be ladled out on to paper for sale. It was mucky stuff in the summer and rather hard in the winter. Tea and sugar were also carried in bulk and had to be weighed for sale.

The main fur resource was musquash (muskrat) and the previous year, due to competition, the buying price had gone up to $5, with a consequent loss when sold at the auction in London, England.

In October, I came down with typhoid fever and was lucky

to get out to hospital in The Pas on the last boat before freeze-up.

By January 1928, I was back to Cumberland House, and in March was sent out with Solomon Ballantyne, a Métis, by dog team with trade goods to visit the trappers and buy their musquash. We made two more trips that spring, the last one by canoe. However, a bootlegger was ahead of us and some of the camps we visited on this last trip were full of drunk trappers. We bought "rats" that spring for $2 top grade.

Ralph Butchart,
Lac du Bonnet, Manitoba

THE BEST DEAL THEY EVER MADE

My husband and I purchased the little store in Worcester, Saskatchewan in 1929. The previous owner made a voluntary assignment to his creditors and we were able to purchase the contents for 40¢ on the dollar, a total of $1300.

This sum of money we did not have, as we were newly married. My husband was one of the two grain buyers in the hamlet, and we hoped his salary plus our profits from the store would eventually pay for the merchandise. In the meantime, we approached three fairly wealthy and amiable-looking farmers with a request for the loan of the $1300. We were prepared to return this sum in the form of groceries until the debt was paid.

They all came through, two of them with $500 each and the third with $300. Over the next six years they declared over and over again it was the best deal they ever made. In the drought-stricken area of southern Saskatchewan, they alone in the district could live well, with or without the relief orders granted them.

Our store was a typical country store. DEALER IN THE NEEDS OF EVERYBODY was blazoned on its south wall. And we did mean everybody, for we had everything . . . a full line of groceries, a good hardware section, shoes and fabrics, work clothes, twine, flour, pump for gasoline, gas delivery for farm machinery, cameras and film, confectionery, valve insides, valves, light bulbs, to name a few. We also housed the post office and looked after the mail.

During our period in this business, we improved amenities

of the town by buying and installing a delco plant so we had electric lights; and installed a freezer from which we dispensed ice cream, and so encouraged the localities to forego their Saturday-night trips into the city of Weyburn, where they would undoubtedly buy their week's supply of groceries at less cost. Organizing ball games on Saturday nights assisted in discouraging this practice to a certain extent.

Mr. and Mrs. John Ringstrom,
Worcester, Saskatchewan

THAT URGE TO GO WEST

*I*n 1918, my father, Dave Bradshaw, wanted to come out west. My brother and foster brother had come out first, and my parents wanted to come see them. So Dad bought a 490 Chev and we motored all the way from Brantford, Ontario to Coronation, Alberta . . . my father, mother, brother and myself. That was quite a trip. I was 18.

We left on the fourth of July in our Chevrolet touring car. No trunk or anything. Oh it was an adventure! Came out to investigate. Before Father was married he had been out west a couple of times and he always had that urge to go back.

We crossed at Windsor and went to Kalamazoo, Michigan and stopped to get a map, skirted around Chicago and came into Canada at Emerson, then on up to Winnipeg where my father had a brother, an engineer. We were one of the first to come out this far by car. Nothing more than a flat tire or two and broken springs. The u-bolts would break and then we'd have to wire it up or we'd go to a blacksmith shop. I can't remember now where we got gas.

In Brantford, Father had the Cockshutt agency. When we came here in 1919, he bought this farm down at Haneyville. Haneyville was there before Coronation, but the railway by-passed it. My husband, Jack, was here before the railway, so he remembers how it was:

"When this country was settling up before Dave Bradshaw came, before the railways came, people with foresight might go out and say, 'This is just about where the town is going to be, so we'll build a little country store here.' And sometimes they were pretty near right. But these people at Haneyville were miles away."

A lot of the buildings were moved from Haneyville to Coronation. But the livery barn and the Stopping House were still on this farm my parents had. Then when the "dirty thirties" came, it was too much for them. So, in 1933, Father bought this store at Federal from Gus Meyer . . . Gus was the one who built it.

That store was built out of packing boxes. Coffee came in packing boxes, I think tea did too. Most things came in packing boxes. The inside was lined with cardboard, covered over with the wide-rolled kraft paper, and then they took thin lath and wrapped the paper around it and that was nailed up in a checkerboard pattern.

There was a big pot-bellied stove in it. In those days there was cheap coal from the mines at Castor . . . the seams were close to the surface and easy to mine. People came in and sat around at night, particularly the bachelors who had no other social life. The card table was there, always set up by the stove, and they'd play cards to all hours.

Greta (Bradshaw), Jack and Bob Hallett,
Coronation, Alberta

HOW THE BELLS DID RING

*W*e were a bride and groom. All of us settlers came in from the east, from Red Deer; the train, loaded with settlers effects, took eight hours. When we arrived at eight o'clock at night, we came up in the mud and rain from the station to the Mount View Hotel.

This Englishman had this team and a little wagon and the seats went down the long way, built out over the wheels, and he had old horse blankets on the darn thing, and I looked at Joe and here I had on my lovely blue suit and big hat. Anyway the old horses started to kick. You know you're supposed to have your hands together when you drive but this Englishman had his hands out like this . . . . And here the horses were kicking up their heels, and I thought the whole front of the wagon was going to be kicked off. As the wheels would turn they would grind on this plank he had stretched out to sit on. He charged 50¢ for lifting people up to the hotel.

The ground floor at the hotel was being renovated and they were making rooms. So we occupied a room with a partition up so high, the rest of it was open. For a bride and groom! And no toilet facilities; we had to go outside. They did give us a can.

Joe had been here six months already and had gone out to get his bride. After the war, the government gave the army boys a half section of land in this area for $10, and Joe was one of them. So after we got through with the room with the funny partition, a friend from out on a homestead came to pick us up with horses and a buggy. First we went down to get an order from Killick's store. It was rainy and Killick had one of these umbrellas provided by the Royal Crown Soap Company for the delivery rig to use. It was eight feet wide, white and red panels with Royal Crown Soap advertised on it. He gave us this umbrella to protect my fine new hat.

There was a ferry across the Saskatchewan River for the homesteaders. But there wasn't a made road at all; we just went in two tracks and we kept going into these great dips. In one dip our homesteader friend had the lines held pretty tight and he fell right out of the buggy.

Some fellow had already homesteaded our land, cleared five acres and built this little shack, but we think he must have gone to the war and got himself killed. We took our big umbrella into the shack with us. After a few nights, a herd of neighbour's cattle came to our cleared five acres of land. And they had bells on and all night long they would ring those bells.

Joe went out and poked at them with this umbrella and complained that they didn't pay any attention: "They would just look around and get down to eating the good grass and ringing their bells. So then I had the idea I could do better. I opened the umbrella up quickly. And the whole caboodle, they all turned tail and galloped off into the bush with the bells ringing. Just stampeded."

You could hear them for miles away. When he opened the umbrella, the bells how they did ring! We lived out there two months before we packed up and came into town. We had both worked for the Hudson's Bay Company and we were going to go to Edmonton and get a job. Joe was English and had never been on a homestead in his life. Most of the homesteaders hadn't. Most of them packed up and left. It was hopeless without machinery. Poor land, good for pasture and raising cattle. The government put a lid on homesteading shortly after, and it all went back to Crown Land.

"So when Jenny and I went into Killick's store on our way
to Edmonton, he asked me how we were doing. When I told
him we were packing it in, going to Edmonton, he said, 'You've
got a job here tomorrow if you want it.'

"So we stayed. I worked with Killick until 1923 and then
started on my own. We stayed and ran a store here for 54 years
until 1977."

Jenny and Joe Cony,
Rocky Mountain House, Alberta

BUILT OUT OF NOTHING

*A*ctually, he built the store out of nothing. 1936. It was really
hard times. Everybody was out of a job and unemployment was
just terrible. During the winter of '35-'36, he worked on the ice-
gang putting up ice for all around the country, and when that
was finished there was no prospect of work.

He used to have a farm too, until he lost his farm, dried out
in the bad years. Drought, just year after year. He'd lose his
crop. And sometimes hail . . . in the late twenties. There was
just no way to keep on.

I had two older brothers, one finishing high school. Dad
. . . his name was John McGarry . . . said to the boys, "Well,
when you can't get work you have to make work for yourself."
He had worked for a storekeeper in Lorlie a bit and he had
experience working for lumber companies, selling lumber. And
there was an elevator man in Finney who had a post office in
his elevator. And they decided not to allow that anymore, didn't
want elevator men to have the post office. So Dad had a chance
to get it. Then he thought if he could have a little store as well,
that would help.

So he didn't have money to get lumber to build a store or
post office. But he used to build boats and he had odds and
ends of lumber, so he got enough to build the framework of a
little shack. I remember, he would line the insides of the shack
with anything he could get: cardboard, tar-paper, anything to
keep out the cold. Later on when they tore that place down,
they got a big surprise when they found what was under. There
wasn't any lumber to salvage . . . just the framework. My
mother would cover it over with wallpaper when he built a part
on the back to live in.

STOVES, HARDWARE. PAINTS,
S, TINWARE, SILVERWARE,
RY GOODS, BOOTS & SHOES,
GRICULTURAL IMPLEMENTS,
NDER TWINE &c.

P.G. TOWNS

HIGHEST PRICES PAID,
BUTTER, EGGS, POULTRY
DRESSED HOGS, LARD

C TOWNS
W'SHIP TREASURER

OUR MOTTO.
BEST GOODS, AT
REASONABLE PRICES

GROCERIES, SEEDS, PATENT
MEDICINES, SCHOOL BOOKS,
CROCKERY, GLASSWARE,
HATS, CAPS, RUGS, CLOCKS,
WEDDING PRESENTS &c.

SALADA TEA
G. TOWNS

PUBLIC WEIGH SCALE

35

When he first wanted to start the store and he didn't have any money, he got in touch with the wholesalers in Melville and Yorkton and asked if they were interested in giving him a start. They weren't too interested.

He said, "Well, give me two dozen chocolate bars and some tobacco (it was more tobacco than cigarettes in those days), and when I get those sold, if everything's OK, I'll maybe get some more." By that time he might have some money from the post office. Anyway, that was his first order, some tobacco and some chocolate bars, and only two dozen, if you can imagine.

And then he decided he would build an icehouse . . . just a shed . . . digging it into the ground and putting in the straw the way they knew how to do it in the old days. So he put ice in there, and then he would order pop. And he built a little icebox to put the ice in to keep the pop cold.

As time went on he got more chocolate bars, and he began to get groceries and to get things that working men would want, like gloves and coveralls and work-socks, and gradually he got into hardware, like staples (people were always needing staples to fix their fences) and nails and paint. And he made a deal with the bakery to sell bread. Until he had just about everything that people would need. A general store.

Corine (McGarry) Stillborn,
Finnie, Saskatchewan

THE SHORTILLS OF BALLINAFAD

*T*he Shortills who run the Ballinafad store have been in Ballinafad since the first John Shortill came from Tipperary in the early 1800s.

He was a man of great perseverance. He loved a girl in Tipperary, but the mother of the girl he loved, despised him. This determined widow decided to take her family of daughters to Canada and away from Shortill.

When the long ocean voyage was over and the ship docked, the weary women walked down the gangplank; there on the quay was Shortill waiting for them. Needless to say, he married his girl.

Rita Shortill,
Ballinafad, Ontario

CHAPTER THREE

THE STORE'S COMMUNITY

The store's relationship with its community was both economic and intimate. Church, school, grist mill, lumber mill, cheese factory, blacksmith shop and hotel came together where two roads met or, as in Young's Point, Ontario, where road and water met.

A country store never existed alone. It might sit solitary where two roads cross, but it has always been absolutely dependent on a network of people. At the very least, it needs a surrounding of farms; over the years it has thrived best where other institutions and industries come together . . .

This scene of early morning activity ▷
is at the Warminster Cheese
Factory near Peterborough,
Ontario. Often the farmer's way
home led past the village store and,
more often than not, he stopped.
For an hour or two each morning,
the "milk trade" could make the
store a busy place.

*churches, schools, hotels, cheese factories, mills, blacksmith
and tinsmith shops, cabinetmakers, shoemakers and carriage
builders workshops.*

*In pioneer days it made sense for a store to locate near a
mill where people already came with grain or timber. The
settler usually left half of the flour or the lumber as payment
to the miller. Sometimes the miller became a storekeeper,
taking more of the flour or the lumber in exchange for tea and
sugar and crockery or whatever the settler needed. Grist and
lumber mills were soon followed by carding and fulling mills,
oat mills, planing mills and shingle mills, as the small
industrial village began its sporadic growth.*

*To get his grain to the mill . . . and to do any heavy work
on his land . . . a settler needed a beast of burden, an ox at
first, later a horse. It is not surprising that every tiny village
had its blacksmith shop, and that every smithy held a special
position in the community as a talented artistic muscleman
who worked in iron. Cobourg, Ontario (today a town of
20 000) had 22 blacksmith shops in 1857.*

*Cheese factories came later than blacksmith shops. In
Ontario's Oxford County, the first cheese factories appeared in
1864 and began to take cheese production out of the home.
Eventually, butter would be made in creameries. The farmer
would have less produce for barter at the local store but more
money. Cheese factories played a major role in the change-
over to a rural cash economy.*

*In the last 30 years, cheese factories, like blacksmith
shops, have done a disappearing act as production became
centralized in larger factories. In the 1950s, a great many
factories went up in smoke, arousing suspicions of arson
among neighbours and insurance companies. The small cheese
factories which survive today produce superior cheese prized
by city dwellers, who enjoy a drive to the country for Pine
Grove or Warkworth or Black River Cheese.*

*Only memories remain of the cheese factory as an early
morning gathering place when all the farm wagons in the
community rolled in with their milk. Each morning the
"factory" rivalled the country store as a gossip exchange. Like
the blacksmith shop, it was preferred by some men because*

there were no women around. On the other hand, you needed good weather to sit on a wagon or sleigh and "chew the fat" with neighbours sitting on theirs. When a blizzard blew, you just emptied your milk cans fast and got on back to the stove in the store.

Early inns and hotels appeared everywhere in Canada as small communities began to grow. Sometimes inn and store were one building, with one proprietor. Large two-storeyed stores which exist today, can often be recognized as early hotels. Where inns were not actually serving as stores, they sometimes were involved in merchandising when travelling salesmen rented a room to display their wares to local storekeepers.

Inns and taverns came in all shapes, sizes and degrees of dirt. They could be places of warmth and cleanliness and gracious hospitality, but often they were vermin-infested, draughty and noisy, places where sleep was almost impossible and food was sometimes inedible. Some were low-down drinking houses; some were temperance houses established as an alternative to the taverns that were too prevalent, particularly in logging areas. (One early traveller described the Bobcaygeon Road in Ontario as "one long drawn-out tavern".)

This big yellow store at Gondola Point near Saint John, N.B. was built as a hotel. The hotel was made into a store 35 years ago. "When grandfather got too old to run the hotel, he started a little tiny store, and then it grew."

*Taverns were often meeting places for political parties,
sites for militia parades, and places where dances, elections or
courts were held. At least one tavernkeeper hosted church
services in the hall over his driving shed.*

*When a community had built itself a church, it was really
a community . . . secure, hopeful of permanence and growth.
Apart from the solace and strength which early churches gave
to a pioneer people, they soon became social centres, meeting
places on Sundays when the stores were closed, and gathering
places for Christmas concerts and turkey suppers and
strawberry socials.*

*As changing times brought iron rails, the station and
station agent became important additions to communities not
bypassed by the railroad. In western Canada, the town was
usually built after the railway at a designated town site set
apart by the CPR, or later the CNR. If you were there too
soon and got missed, you moved your town, lock, stock and
barrel. In Alberta, Harvey Beaubier first lived in a town
named Cleverhill . . . a name that will disappear with old-
timers like himself, for Cleverhill had to move, and became the
new town of Champion.*

*As the West was settled, the skyscape contained one insti-
tution not seen in Eastern communities. The grain elevator
stood bold and beautiful against the sky, like a promise of
bountiful harvest and an exclamation point for the railway
which carried its grain to the rest of the world. Visible at great
distances on the flat prairie landscape, the elevator was often
the beacon which guided a lost foot-traveller or a lone horse
rider home.*

*In Atlantic Canada, the wharf or dock or stage was a
community centre in itself. In areas where there were no
roads, activity centred around the waterfront. In some Newfoundland communities, there were seal-oil plants and lobster-
canning plants, usually owned by the merchant who had
contacts in St. John's and who "was everything to everybody"
in the outport.*

*In whatever small community, in whatever part of
Canada, whatever else was going on, the country store, the
place where you could trade what you didn't want and buy
what you did, sat at the centre of its small universe.*

SATURDAY NIGHT IN A CO-OP TOWN

*T*he word Co-op was something like Church in our hometown. Co-op was the thing . . . a marvelous idea.

Remember how they used to keep the Co-op store open until 12 o'clock on Saturday nights, and all the farmers came into town? In those days the customer stood on one side of the counter and the orders were filled on the other side. And somebody would carry the boxes out to your car. When it got really busy, some of the Co-op directors would come in and work. There was a wonderful spirit among the people. No one got paid anything for doing it.

In summertime on a Saturday night, the band used to play on the bandstand. You could hear the music all over town. People would walk up and down the streets. In wintertime, we would go down to the rink. We curled and skated then to the same band.

Mr. Neeley was one of the farmers who would come into the store and help; but Mrs. Neeley would park her car in front of the store there. She'd get there early and get a place and she'd stay there until 12 o'clock. And she'd visit with all the people walking up and down. If you wanted to know if somebody was in town, you went and asked her and she told you whether they were.

Vera and Maldwyn Hughes
and Florence Maynes,
Lemberg, Saskatchewan

ELECTION DAY

*E*very time there was an election, people would almost get into a brawl. We voted in the town hall. My father was a dyed-in-the-wool Conservative and this other old fellow, a customer of ours, was a Grit. They never got along, not for any particular reason; they just rubbed each other the wrong way. So every time an election was on, this old fellow would go up to the polling booth and he'd sit and he'd wait all day until my Dad got away from the store and came up to vote. And as soon as my Dad voted, he'd get up and he'd vote and say loudly, ''There's a vote I killed!''

Jean (Weir) Drimmie,
Lang, Ontario

CONFEDERATION OR NOT

Most people in Rocky Harbour were in favour of Newfoundland joining Canada. At that time in the late forties I was working in the lumber woods and the girls were running the store. I had a crew in the woods and when Joey Smallwood asked us to send in names of men in favour of Confederation, I had nine names in favour and one against.

I sent the names to St. John's. That's when they were trying to get Confederation on the ballot paper. The government didn't want Confederation on the ballot paper at all. But Smallwood and Bradley, they was fighting for Confederation. So the government found there were so many people in favour that they had to put it on the ballot paper.

Gordon Shears,
Rocky Harbour, Newfoundland

Churches welded a community together while they brought it solace and a sense of being "Nearer My God to Thee". This one looks out to sea at Twillingate, Newfoundland.

A CATHOLIC JOINED THE PARADE

*T*here was never much trouble between Catholics and Protestants in the area. At one time Catholics and Protestants used the same two-room school. On the 12th of July, a few Orangemen used to get out the fifes and drums and play "The Protestant Boys" in front of the Catholic church. One day, the local barber, who was a Catholic, borrowed a big bass drum and joined the parade which turned out to be the last one.

Jerry Raper,
Cargill, Ontario

Lumber mills often gathered a community around them. The Selkirk family ran this one at Blytheswood near Leamington in southwestern Ontario.

HOSPITALITY

Very, very lovely people on the Magdalen Islands. I got stuck one time in a storm travelling for DeBloise Brothers Groceries. The driver couldn't come that day but he told me to take his car. It started to storm. I got to the point-of-no-return about 25 miles out. I didn't see a thing for a long time. But I knew I had passed a house, so I left the car there and walked back and I was there for two days.

The people who would take me in during a storm would never take any money. They used to roll their own cigarettes, so I would send them tobacco after. They couldn't do enough for me. They'd be giving me the wine or the liquor, but if other company came in they wouldn't give them any. I was special because I was a guest from off the Island.

When I would go into the stores, if the store had ten customers they stood there and waited until the storekeeper finished with me. Because I was from off the Island.

But they are very clannish people. If there would be a wedding . . . maybe a storekeeper's daughter . . . they would close down the stores and all the travellers on the Island would be invited. We'd get a gift and we'd go. It would start in the morning and go on for a couple of days. The tables would be set up for two days. Drinks too, but no excess.

There was one chap from Quebec there selling shoes and he said it was foolish and he wouldn't go. They boycotted him, called up all the stores and said that he wouldn't go, said he didn't think they were good enough. They said, "Don't buy from him!"

He had to go home. The company had to send another man down.

Gerald Nantes,
Magdalen Islands, Quebec

45

REALLY A WONDERLAND

*T*he West in those days was really a wonderland, because you never knew what to expect. And everything was wild, really wild!

Cattle you know, they'd never see a person on foot. And if they'd see you walking, you know, they were right after you. I was chased one night by a bunch of cattle when I was about 17. As luck would have it, I fell into a cattle trail, an old cow trail about so deep. I rolled into this and they run right on over me, went right on. Maybe 50 or 60 of them. And it was pitch dark.

They went in the direction between me and my home. I laid there for a long time, listening, wondering if they'd moved on past there, so I could get home. Apparently they'd kept right on going. So I got home. I'd walk a little bit and then I'd stop and listen. Got home about three o'clock in the night.

Another time I walked to Lethbridge, 42 miles. And back. I went down there to get a job. Old McArthur, the railway contractor, was camped on top of the hill there for to build this railway. This was in the spring and it was raining. Oh boy, it was a wet spring. He had his tents on the hill on the south side of the river. I went in and hit him up for a job.

"My golly, boy. I got fellows here I've fed for six months. I can't let them go and give you a job." So I fooled around there for a while and couldn't find nothing.

But goin' down, the rain shower came up about 15 miles this side of Lethbridge. And I was hungry and I came up to this fine big house and barn. And I thought, by golly, I had enough on me to buy a loaf of bread. So I knocked on the door. And it was an old German couple. One of them had a butcher knife and the other one had a big meat fork.

I commenced to laugh and it was quite a while before I could make them understand . . . they talked to one another in German . . . finally I showed them "hungry" and "bread". So they got a loaf of bread and they wouldn't take no money for it. So then I had nothing to drink, and quite a job making them understand I needed some water. Finally she goes in and come out with a big pitcher of milk.

I stopped at the same place coming back and paid for my lunch. After that we'd always stop there when we were hauling grain or goods for the store. We christened their place Hotel De Dumpling because she always gave us dumplings.

Harvey Beaubier,
Champion, Alberta

MATTAGAMI HOUSE

I was born at Mattagami House, a Hudson's Bay Company Post on the Mattagami River southwest of today's Timmins. I was one of the ten children of James Miller who came from Scotland about 1875 to run the post there for 40 years.

There was no Timmins then; we got our supplies from Biscotasing on the CPR, 100 miles to the southwest, and we took our furs out to there by canoe. Before the railway (1885), furs had to go out by the Mattagami all the way to Moose Factory on James Bay, by canoe. It would take a month going down and another month to bring supplies back.

The Indians would camp around the post in summertime, exchanging their furs for sugar and tea and flour and tobacco. They bought smoking tobacco in a plug. They would carve off a bit, rub it in their hands, then smoke it in their pipes.

The furs had to go out in June. My sisters and brothers and I would help beat the beaver skins with sticks to take the dust off before they were put under a press and then into special boxes made by Father. Other less-valued skins would be sewed into canvas for the outward journey.

It was my job to make bread in a large outdoor oven; then I sold it in the store for 50¢ a loaf. Sometimes I would help cut moose meat and hang it over a fire. Charlotte and Beth and I also became trappers, taking muskrat and marten and fisher. Other times we would take a rifle and go after moose.

I can clearly remember a trip I made by sleigh out to Bisco 70 years ago. Charlotte and I had set a trap with a moose head for bait, and in it we found a very ferocious fisher. I hit at it with an axe. When I missed, the angry fisher almost got free. Charlotte took the axe and did not miss. But on the way downhill with our prey, I fell on the axe and cut my finger to the bone. Bleeding profusely, I made it back to the post. But Father did not like the look of it and next morning hitched the dog team, wrapped me in blankets, and took me overland 65 miles to a doctor at Bisco.

I was married by the time the Ontario Hydro's new dam on the Mattagami flooded Mattagami House. This was around 1915. My father tried to stop the flooding and save his post, but government officials turned a deaf ear. The graves around the post were moved across the lake. The store and storehouses were emptied of their stock, the contents of our house taken away, and one of the early fur-trading posts of the north disappeared beneath the rising waters of Mattagami Lake.

Jean (Miller) Leach,
Mattagami House, Ontario

PORT HARDY

*W*e both worked on Vancouver Island at the Port Hardy Supermarket, owned by the Dong Chong Company . . . a Chinese family. They had three stores, one at Alert Bay, one at Port Hardy and one at Port Alice. Very fine people. Very good people to work for. We were there until 1976.

When we went to Port Hardy in the early sixties, it was a forest industry town and a mission town and semi-isolated. No highway in. Just a logging road. Or the ferry from Bear Cove to Kelsey Bay. When it rained, that logging road was something else. We got a lot of rain, but not all the time. You got used to it. You'd plan a picnic and you'd go anyway, whether it was raining or not.

At the time we lived there, we really enjoyed it. But once the mines started coming in, you got your transient workers and you'd just have problems on top of problems. Then when the highway was finished, it became a boom town.

Before that it served the outlying areas. The government boats would come in to the wharf and radiotelephone us to get the garbage trucks and water and bring down their grub. And BC Telephone had a station up on an island. They would radiotelephone in their order and we'd even pick up their booze, and it was all flown out to them. Most of the camp orders were done in the same fashion. For a while we had the helicopter come in right behind the store at five in the morning, but some people got a little upset, so then we had to take the supplies to the airport. And we would grub up all the pleasure boats from Hawaii, going through to Alaska.

One interesting thing to see was the last of the whaling. They stopped it in 1961. It was a BC Packers operation and they used to bring a number of Japanese over to process the whales. The whale products would go to Japan, some of it for fertilizer, the whale oil for food products. The plant was in Coal Harbour. Coal Harbour was a very smelly place to be around.

For the first four years, everything came into Port Hardy by boat . . . food, hardware, literally everything. It was nothing to get up at two in the morning and go down and unload a boat that was late coming in. Oh, you'd hear it! You'd hear them honking coming around the bend.

Al Jackson,
Port Hardy, British Columbia

HOUSE-HAULING

*W*e used to move homes across the ice. House-hauling we called it. Somebody would have a house, say on the north island, and want to move it here to Twillingate. They'd go around and canvass, perhaps a week ahead, that they were going to haul the house on a certain day. They'd go from door to door with a stick about so long to bang on the door. If you saw a man coming with a stick that long in the winter, you knew there was a house-hauling. Everyone would turn up. You looked forward to it.

The man having the house hauled would come to the store and buy so many sacks of flour, so much biscuits and so on. He would get his neighbours to help cook it all up, cakes and things. It was a party and you would have your meals there for two days.

We wouldn't close the store, but if it happened to be a holiday, we'd get there. When we were youngsters we would run away from school to get to a house-haul. And after the older ones ate, we youngsters would go in and eat. We were always welcome, too.

Two big logs would be put underneath, tapered in the front. They would be bolted to the house, tied. I've heard them called *slippers* and I've heard them called *sleepers*. There would be six or seven inches of snow on the ice. Sometimes they had enough men to plough the snow ahead of them.

They would use a four-inch-round line and there would be a

line of men maybe 500 feet long. Sometimes the men had a short piece of rope which they would make fast to the big rope. The same way you'd launch a boat. That's how they hauled seals too; they hooked it into the seal and onto their shoulders and took a twist around their arm.

Sometimes they would get the house part way home and come to a little hill and not have enough men, so they would have to leave it there. The men would go back to their homes all around the island . . . walk, it was all walking then . . . to bring more men back the next day. Send out the word, "We need more help!"

They had a foreman and he would lose his voice from bawling before the house was landed. When the house got stuck or they wanted to start it, they would put a pry under the nose of it and they would sing "The Johnny Poker". It's a Newfoundland song for hauling a boat, or hauling anything.

> Oh me Johnny Poker,
> We will move this heavy Joker,
> And it's only Johnny Poker . . . Ho!

When they say "Ho!", everybody pulls. They wouldn't all hear him, but they'd see his arms go up with the "Ho!" and they'd all pull.

The house has to come. Something has to come. Maybe they'll have to sing it half a dozen times, but eventually they'll get it.

Bill Ashbourne and Herb Gillett,
Twillingate, Newfoundland

HOW THEY GOT A SCHOOL IN CHEMINIS

*A*bout 1926, there were seven or eight young people there that needed a school. Leo Copp, who became principal of the Teachers' College in Peterborough, was then the Inspector of Public Schools in that part of the country. He used to travel on foot, by railway, in airplanes and with dog teams. And he was well loved. I don't think there was anybody my father liked any better than that man.

Father was the storekeeper and he wrote to him, and he came and said, "You people build the school, make a place where the children can be, and I'll see what I can do to get a grant."

The children of this Bridgenorth, Ontario school have learned the fine art of growing a garden.

So they built the log-cabin school out of nice, beautiful spruce. There was a chap by the name of Hall, a railway agent. And N.J. Boylen was one of them . . . he became a millionaire. They all pulled together and built the school. Then the government of Ontario gave them a grant of $1000 for a teacher. Teachers got $80 to $85 a month in those days.

There were no school taxes because it was unorganized land, except for a few mining claims that had been patented before 1918 when you got all mineral and timber rights to the land. They taxed those claims at $6 or $9 each, so they got maybe a couple hundred dollars, plus the thousand from the Department of Education through Leo Copp.

Then they put an ad in the papers: TEACHER WANTED AT CHEMINIS. Cheminis was a godforsaken place for a young man or woman, so they offered $1250. They got bushels of applications. One night, my father and Boylen and Hall went through those applications and came across one they liked, a young man of 23, Percy Hamilton from Millbrook, Ontario.

But with $1250 and a few other expenses, they were over their budget. Where to find another $200? Somebody had a bright idea! The Power Corporation of Canada had a big power line going through the Township of McGarry to the Noranda mines, and our school section was known as "The Township of McGarry School Section". So somebody had the idea to assess the Power Corporation of Canada for $200. They didn't know whether it was legal or illegal and they didn't care. So that was in September, and by the end of October they got a cheque for $200 from the Power Corporation and they were all set!

Albert Emond,
Cheminis, Ontario

BUILD A HOSPITAL

*T*he hospital was a godsend. Before that, people on Bonne Bay, Newfoundland died and didn't know what they died of. TB was raging; whole families died out with TB. My parents lost two little boys with diphtheria; one died one day; one the next. My mother died when I was 14 and I don't know what she died of.

My father went five times for the doctor, and he wouldn't come. At last my uncle got him, a week before she died. He went back and sent her some medicine and was heard to say, "I'll make those Rocky Harbour people know who I am." She took the medicine that evening, went into a coma and never came out of it.

My uncle had whiskers and he tasted a bit, and it dropped on his whiskers and burned them. The lighthouse-keeper sent it away and had it analysed . . . it was 90 percent poison . . . iodine or something like that.

The doctor was a drunkard and a drunkard is a crazy man. He was the only doctor around. At that time . . . 60 years ago . . . there was a hospital in St. Anthony (The Grenfell Mission) 250 miles north and another in St. John's, 500 miles away.

In 1937, in November, I got this message from a Dr. McDermott from St. John's to meet him on the coast boat to go to Port Saunders up the coast, and build a hospital. I'd never heard tell of him before.

When we were trying to get to Port Saunders, this Dr. McDermott and I were stormbound for two days in Bonne Bay. I said to him, "We've been trying to get a hospital here for 50 years." We were anchored out in the bay, so I showed him Woody Point where there was a doctor. "Across the bay at Norris Point there's 500-600 people. Six miles out there's Rocky Harbour with the same amount. Twelve miles west there's Trout River. Eight miles up the harbour there's Lomond. And all we've got in our settlements for medical attention, is a midwife. What would a doctor do today in this storm to get across the bay?"

"He couldn't do it."

"In spring and fall this bay is full of ice and there's a month or two that you can't cross at all."

He said, "Well, if you can build a hospital at Port Saunders for the $4000 we got cut out for it, then we'll start one here in Bonne Bay."

And we did. We finished the Port Saunders one in '38 and then in 1939 we built the one here in Bonne Bay. There was 90 000 feet of lumber given free by local people, and 7500 hours of free labour, and $2000 from the government for roofing, paint, doors and a lighting plant. I was the builder and the only one paid. I got 40¢ an hour.

So we done it.

James Shears,
Rocky Harbour, Newfoundland

GETTING TOGETHER IN PLUMAS

*I*n the small Manitoba town of Plumas, there were 300 people, but seven churches. People of different nationality . . . German, Ukrainian, Scottish and Irish . . . had come there and established their different religious faiths. Eventually they looked at each other and said "We don't need all these churches," and they got it down to three: Lutheran, Methodist and Presbyterian.

Then in the 1920s, along came the movement for Church Union. All over Canada, Methodists and Presbyterians were joining to become the United Church of Canada. In Plumas the

Methodists met and voted unanimously to join with the Presbyterians. Right away the Presbyterians met and voted unanimously not to join the Methodists.

So the Methodists met again. This time they voted to all become Presbyterian. The following Sunday they all turned up at the Presbyterian church and there they stayed.

Three years later, the Presbyterians of Plumas took another vote on Church Union. This time they voted to join. So in 1928, they became part of the United Church of Canada.

Bill Wells,
Plumas, Manitoba

This attractive grist mill, restored by the Otonabee Conservation Authority, is central to the village of Lang. It keeps company now with Lang Century Village, a re-created 1820-1900 village.

CHAPTER FOUR

BUTTER, EGGS AND GENERAL BARTER

As small communities struggled into being in all parts of Canada, individuals with some imagination saw an alternative to wresting a livelihood directly from the soil. They provided a barter service through which customers could trade grain and potash and butter and eggs for sugar and tea and molasses. Storekeepers forwarded the butter and eggs, potash, sides of pork, furs and hides to markets in Montreal or Halifax or Vancouver and, with the cash received, brought in goods which the settlers needed. Between storekeeper and farmer, little cash changed hands at first.

The stories that came down about butter and eggs and other bartered items tend to be negative. It's the bad eggs that get remembered, as well as the butter that was rancid. But there is little doubt that the system worked. Where actual markets were far away, or the farmer lacked the marketing know-how, the storekeeper was acting as a go-between. The farmer could take payment in store goods before the wood, furs or fish ever reached the actual consumer.

For farm women, butter-and-egg barter had special significance. They chased around after chickens because the egg money was theirs, *their first independence in days long predating "women's liberation". They churned extra butter for the same reason.*

Often they walked their produce to town. One story tells of a Scottish immigrant woman who would walk several miles to the local store with her eggs and butter. Plunking them down on the counter, she would say the only non-Gaelic words she knew: "Dougal will come r-round with the English."

Mrs. Lily Hudson, now living in the Bancroft area of Ontario, remembers that her grandmother would walk 13 miles to bring her eggs to the store. She would get 8¢ a dozen for the eggs and have to stay overnight. On a good day in May, that walk may have been a rare delight and her stay in town a taste of freedom and adventure. At other times, drenched by rain or blown by a storm, her walk must have been a nightmare.

Barter had its problems for the storekeeper too. "Handling" the bartered item was always time-consuming. If it was a bulky item, such as grain, he had to have a team and wagon or sleigh to cart it away, as well as a ready market. If it was a perishable item, such as butter or eggs, he needed a wary eye before he accepted it; then he had to store it in a cool place, and he had to cart it carefully to a larger centre.

In northern Canada, the Hudson's Bay Company built its fur-trading empire on barter. The first stores of the North were posts set up to barter with a people that had no money, but who had valuable furs which could be converted to cash once they reached England. In return, the Company could give the Indians sugar, tea, tobacco, guns and cooking pots, colourful plaids, trinkets and beads. When an Indian trapper entered the store at Cumberland House or Mattagami House with a winter's catch of furs, the wonders of the white man's world were his.

In most parts of Canada, barter was on its way out in the 1920s. But it made a grand recovery in the desperate 1930s, when money virtually disappeared from rural areas. Imaginative trading between storekeeper and customer, and between individual farmers, was all that kept the community fed, dressed and warm.

Barter remained an important way of doing business in northern Canada long after southern stores dealt only in cash. Here, furs are exchanged for pablum and coffee and canned foods at Coppermine in the Northwest Territories in 1950.

EGG YOLK ALL OVER

My grandmother claimed hers was the first white family in the Gatineau . . . came up here around 1810. They came to the Hull area in 1801 with Philemon Wright. My great-grandfather and two brothers were millwrights and built the first mills at Chaudière Falls.

I started storekeeping with my father in 1923. In the early days there was a lot of farming on small plots, usually 100 acres, partly bush. People would bring in butter and eggs. My father would never turn away butter. One guy brought in a pot of butter and dumped it out with the buttermilk all sour and smelling up the store; that stuff wouldn't even make axle grease.

We never made any money on butter and eggs, but you had to do it. I once took 300 dozen eggs all the way to Hull (36 km) when the flood was up, in low gear all the way. By the time I got there, egg yolk was running all over.

Charlie Chamberlin,
Wakefield, Quebec

ALL DAY SUNDAY

Dad had the egg-grading station here for years. It was just a service to the customers; he never made anything more than he paid out. I would start grading eggs at 10 o'clock on Saturday night, go to mass Sunday morning, then grade all day Sunday until 10 o'clock at night.

Bill Towns,
Douro, Ontario

THE TRADING GAME

The 1920s were very good years in our Vernon River store. My husband was a trader and a shipper. We shipped for all the farmers, sent it out by rail and sometimes by schooner. We'd handle anything the farmers had to sell . . . potatoes, chickens, eggs. A lot of it was done by barter.

P.E.I. was all mixed farming then; everybody had a little of everything to sell. At Christmas time we were the largest receiver of dressed poultry on the island. Wonderful chickens, six to seven months old, New York dressed (drawn, but with the legs and head left on) and they weighed nine and ten pounds.

We would have a grader come here from Canada Packers on a certain day of the week, and have the people bring them on that day. Sometimes we would have two or three ton a day. A lot of the assembling was done right in the store, or sometimes in the warehouse. The grader brought all the boxes for packing.

Some of the farmers were getting $200 for their chickens, a lot of money in those days. Then they would buy groceries with the money. The Poultry Days would run from the 5th of December to the 15th, so they'd be on the market for Christmas.

The farmers would bring in the potatoes on sleighs or wagons, and they would be loaded into railway cars. When we would fill a car of potatoes, the inspector would come and it would either pass inspection or be turned down. If he found one lot not graded right, he would turn down the whole car and it would have to be regraded. But the men we hired were careful graders and they were proud, so it didn't happen too often.

One year we shipped 105 carloads of potatoes. We had loaders at other stations who would load cars with potatoes and sell fertilizers to the farmers for us. We sold a lot of fertilizer and feed and flour; carloads would come from Winnipeg.

Then my husband would buy cattle from people, or take them on account. A week before he died . . . suddenly in 1946 at age 64 . . . we went for a drive to Charlottetown one night. He asked me to count the cattle in a field, and I counted them and there were 15. "Well," he said, "they're mine. I've been collecting the last few days. I'll give you the book and you can credit them all to their accounts. There's a Swift's Canadian man coming from Charlottetown and the cattle will be hauled in tomorrow."

Another time, we took a horse on account, a race horse. We paid a man to winter it, and it cost us as much as if we had let the account stay unpaid.

Katie MacLeod,
Charlottetown, Prince Edward Island

OF SALT FISH, SAWMILLS, SHIPS AND STORES

I started fishing out of Rocky Harbour when I was nine years old, went full-time when I was 12. Fished until I was 30. Times was so bad, fish was so low in price and scarce. You could only sell codfish by salting and drying it. Lobster had to be put into cans. Salmon had to be salted in barrels or put in cans. All we could get then was about $2.50 for 112 pounds of dried fish. A lot of work to that.

I gave up fishing and had the sawmill, built the store and started building boats. We would put the sawmill in the bush, cut the lumber and saw it in the winter; then, in summer, we would plane it and ship it and sell it. In 1933, we took the lumber to Corner Brook and sold it for $11 a thousand, trade, no cash involved, had to take it up in foodstuffs . . . beef and pork and flour and sugar. Barter business.

We were operating four sawmills and employing men, so we started a store to help pay their wages. We could trade lumber for food and they could get the food at our store and we wouldn't have to pay out cash. Everything would be charged, and labour at the sawmill would go toward payment. Or the fishermen would pay us in fish. It was all on the barter system. If the customers had anything left over coming to them, we would pay them in cash at the end of the season.

A lot of fishermen would build their own boats, but there were a few people who were very good boat builders who might work with them to build a boat, and they'd trade back labour to pay for the boat. Some years I would build four or five fishing boats, 40-45 or 53-55 feet long. I'd rather build a boat than a house.

We used to bring our own groceries in by ship. In 1934, we built a schooner that was 53 feet long, right here at the back of the house. We would carry a load of lumber to Corner Brook in that schooner and bring back all the freight that we wanted. And we would bring freight for other merchants in Bonne Bay and along the coast.

Altogether we had three stores: the first in 1932, then a small one down at the lake, then this one in 1970. We had a big family, and the girls would keep the store while my wife would be busy at home and I'd be at the sawmill or building boats.

Gordon Shears,
Rocky Harbour, Newfoundland

This store at Kingsmill, Ontario, with its false front, wide veranda and hitching post, is typical of early stores, where people came to barter butter and eggs for flour and sugar and tea.

STORE
KINGSMILL
ONT.

GOOD GRACIOUS, MRS. RINGSTROM

*T*he dust storms, the drought, the grasshoppers of the 1930s seriously hampered our venture into merchandising. The municipality's policy of paying a bounty on gopher destruction, in order to protect the scant crop, provided a means of exchange for the farmers of the area. A gopher tail was worth 2¢, several would buy a bag of flour which fed a family for a couple of weeks. Counting those aging gopher tails, before taking them up to the secretary of the municipality for remuneration, required ingenuity.

It was a dismayed grocer's wife who drove up to the secretary's office one day with thousands of gopher tails, which had provided our customers with food, to be told, "Good gracious, Mrs. Ringstrom, we've stopped paying bounty on gopher tails. The municipality is broke."

Mr. and Mrs. John Ringstrom,
Worcester, Saskatchewan

TRADING COD OIL FOR CALICO

*I*n the early years of this century, a fisherman didn't make enough to buy his outfit, so we got our salt and food and fishing gear and oil clothes and big boots on credit at the store. Then we would dry our fish and take it to the store at Woody Point . . . it was sold by the quintal (112 pounds) . . . and we'd get flour, molasses (no sugar until 1915), salt beef from the mainland at $15 a 200-pound barrel and pork at $20 a barrel.

We were all fishermen. I went fishing when I was eight years old. I had to have a suit of oil clothes and I was too small for ones you could buy, so Mother had to make one. She made it out of what they call shirting and put linseed oil on to make it waterproof. Wipe it on with a brush, a couple of coats until it got seasoned into the cloth. Put it in press under a 200-pound flour barrel, then take it out and dry it. It would be yellow when it was finished, and waterproof.

We would row 20 miles a day to salmon traps, and we would catch lobster and cod. Then it had to be put in cans or salted. We saved the cod oil in those days; it was rendered out for Cod Liver Oil. The men would give the oil to the women, so when we went to Woody Point in the fall to settle up, Mother would have two or three barrels of cod oil at 60¢ a gallon. That was for her to buy what she liked . . . probably a lot of calico to make dresses, and a lot of serge, because she made all our clothes.

First time I went to Woody Point I was 12 years old. I had saved my money all summer and I had 56¢. I bought a hymn book for myself and a set of side combs for my sister's hair. I had 2¢ left and I bought some big chocolates.

James Shears,
Rocky Harbour, Newfoundland

GOT THEM

*T*homas Gilmer from the Valley came in with a basket of eggs. When I counted them out, he lacked two eggs of the even five dozen. He went back outside. I happened to step out into the storehouse for something and I spied him coming out of my henhouse. He came back in and said two eggs had rolled off the basket into the buggy. I paid him for my own two eggs. A good joke was worth the price of two eggs in the 1930s.

Milton Swerdfeger,
Glen Stewart, Ontario

GO GET A COW

*T*he depression was hard times for farmers with milk 52¢ a hundredweight. One farmer owed us about $60 and had no money. He came to the store when I was out and told Mildred he could only pay with a cow. She took his word for the value of the cow. When I got home, she said, "Don't put the truck in, you are to go for a cow I bought."

In those years I took 32 cows "on account", rented them out to farmers and sold them a few years later when prices were better. I also took 12 horses and colts "on account", as well as pigs and turkeys. Very little money changed hands, you traded in things; whatever you could get, you took. One farmer traded me a truckload of potatoes still on the field; I didn't come out ahead on that deal.

One farmer was so low down in the Depression that he brought me the hide of a pig that he lost. I paid him the price of a calf hide to help him out, then buried the pig hide when he left.

Milton Swerdfeger,
Glen Stewart, Ontario

The general store at Century Village, Lang, in Ontario recalls the horse-and-buggy days when the words "barter" and "trade" were synonymous with "country store".

TURKEY CHASE

Alfred Ryley opened the store in the 1850s, and five generations of Ryleys worked in the store until we sold it in 1982.

When I was first married, we used to take in butter and eggs and chickens. Some butter was lovely, but there'd be some lady that didn't make the best butter and what could you do . . . she'd be a good customer, dealing here for years . . . we'd just take the butter in one door and throw it out the other.

Our busiest time was when they used to prepare chickens and bring them in and we'd have to grade them all . . . they'd be all lined down the floor on one side and up the other. Then we had to pack them all at night, because they had to go out on the train or by truck. We used to ship them to Puddy Brothers in Toronto. They'd stay cold enough in the store; that great big barn of a store never got too warm, anyway.

Years ago they used to ship live turkeys in crates on the train. The farmers would bring them in to the store. Bruce used to tell about the turkeys getting away, and they would have quite a job rounding them up.

Helen Ryley,
Bethany, Ontario

GRAND LAYERS

Henry Boyd was our cheesemaker, a gruff, square-built man, slow-spoken but with a twinkle in his eye that showed his sense of humour. All the farmers liked him.

Henry decided he could make extra money with hens, so he bought 25 and in a couple of weeks they had stopped laying altogether. Henry went right on telling the farmers what grand layers his hens were. Finally, one said he would walk over and see these wonderful hens. Henry's wife, Lizzie, had just bought a dozen eggs the day before at our store. While the farmer finished a talk with a neighbour, Henry hurried into the house, got them and put them in the nests. Chester McDermott who was also there with his milk, saw him do it and never said a word at the time. But he told it later in the store.

Milton Swerdfeger,
Glen Stewart, Ontario

66

CASH, CHARGEX OR BLUEBERRIES

*W*hen customers traded in blueberries at Cheminis, my father would give them credit. Every second day they would ship blueberries in 11-quart baskets. All the baskets had to be new and they cost 15¢ each. They came from Gamble-Robinson's in one pile, with covers in another pile and handles in another bundle. People would have to put their own handles on.

The blueberries would be shipped on Monday at two o'clock from Cheminis on the Ontario-Quebec border, 365 miles to Toronto by Ontario Northland Railway. My father would give the people a receipt on a counter cheque book for so many baskets at so much per basket. This would all take shape in three days, Monday to Wednesday. You try to do that today, it would be three weeks!

When customers bought groceries in the summertime at Cheminis, my father used to say, "Will that be cash or blueberries?" So here in Camborne, just in fun, we sometimes say, "Will that be cash, Chargex or blueberries?" A few years ago there was a gas war on and we put out a sign: CASH, CHARGEX OR BLUEBERRIES. But people would drive up and they'd see just that one word, BLUEBERRIES, and in they'd come wanting to buy blueberries. So we had to take down the sign.

Albert Emond,
Camborne, Ontario

NO CHICKENS

*I*n the 1950s all four stores here were doing a good business. People brought in their cans of cream and their eggs. We'd send the eggs to the creamery, too, and they'd grade them. We'd get about half our money back. Some would be good, some wouldn't.

Oh man, we used to have eggs! Many mornings I would come into the store and there's a thousand dozen eggs sitting on the floor. Eight, nine, eleven cents a dozen. I used to stand there and I'd say, "Oh boy, everything is quiet. There's no chickens in them this morning."

John Janowski,
Loon Lake, Saskatchewan

GETTING OUR GOAT

We took chickens on account. And we took a goat! My husband came home in the back of the Cadillac with this goat sitting up chewing away. I can still see it. In my car! He came in the store and he said, "Dear, come and see what I've got in the car."

Oh, I nearly died. I said, "The smell of that, I will die!"

We brought it up here to the house. The boys used to milk it on top of the root cellar and they had a hard time holding it. When Old Chelsea's other store would open up in the morning, our goat would be down there lying on the veranda, or with its two hooves up on the windowsill, looking in the window at them. People didn't bother about it not being tied. It used to play hide-and-go-seek with the kids in front of the root cellar. That was home plate, and the goat would jump and run the same as they were doing.

It was cute, but I didn't like it because of the mess it made. And we couldn't have any flowers; it ate them. We kept it all one summer, then my brother took it to a farmer. When he was leaving, it ran after him behind the van, then it went back and crawled under a shed and it wouldn't come out.

It died in there. We thought it died heartbroken.

Irene (Boland) Lagacé,
Old Chelsea, Quebec

CHAPTER FIVE

PLENTY OF WORK AND A PINCH OF LAUGHTER

There was never any scarcity of work. Putting groceries on the shelf and handing them out to customers was a small part of it. Overrun molasses to clean up, the stove pipes to put up or take down, the stock-taking in January or February added to the fun. In early days, there was the butter to deal with, eggs to grade, hides to handle, coal oil drums to roll in from the barn.

On most jobs, women and men worked together, but there was some division of tasks. In our family, Father handled the flour and feed, cut the glass and sold the harness; Mother could sell wallpaper and Father couldn't; Mother "did the books". A woman often dealt with the wholesale traveller because her man was outside hauling feed, handling binder twine or barbed wire, wood or coal, or putting a new roof on the feedshed. Children often swept the floor, dusted shelves, unpacked groceries, uncrated oranges and "did up" bulk products, such as sugar, dates, raisins and rolled oats.

"Anything you do in a store, it's work," says Mrs. Helen Ryley, whose store closed recently after 133 years in the same

family. "You could work there all day and all night if you wanted to."

Laughter was much scarcer than work. In a community that had to make its own fun, it was an important ingredient for survival, especially during the Depression. At any time it was a valued commodity that made the work lighter, the conversation brighter and the relationship between merchant and customers warmer. Like favourite recipes, the best laughs are passed down and long remembered.

Edwin Guillet's store in Cobourg, Ontario displayed an impressive array of goods.

100-POUND BAGS OF FEED

Sometimes I wondered to myself how I happened to get a business where there was so much heavy work. I put in most of my time handling 100-pound bags of feed. The worst of it was, I only weighed 116 pounds myself. When the seed corn came in each spring, a two-bushel bag weighed 112 pounds.

The main feeds I sold were bran, shorts and middlings. When wheat was ground in the old stone mills, it was sifted in a fine cotton material. Flour was the finest, then middlings, then shorts, finally the bran which was the husks of the wheat kernel. When I first sold at Glen Stewart, bran was only 90¢ a hundredweight.

Flour sold well, as most of the farmers' wives baked their own bread. Middlings were used for pig feed. Bran was used mostly as a tonic for cows and horses. Later on, more specialized feeds came in: chick feed for chickens, laying mash for hens, pig starter and hog grower.

Along with ordinary feeds, I sold gluten feed which was a by-product from the corn at the Canada Starch Factory at Cardinal. I bought by the carload and drew it home 14 miles by truck, a hundred bags per load. One spring, I went two trips a day for three weeks including Saturdays. When I got home there would be glass to cut and things to do in the store, so I would be often until nine o'clock getting the last load off. Then the store would be kept open until 11 every night.

We sold kerosene (coal oil). No roads were ploughed at that time, so we had to put in a supply before the roads blocked. I had 15 45-gallon drums stored out at the barn. I rolled them in and up two skids into a storehouse, three steps high, then had to tip them up on end, which was quite a job.

I also handled coal, wood and cedar posts. The truck bottom was almost to my shoulders and the racks were 52 inches high. Two hundred posts filled the racks, which were almost the length of an eight-foot post. Some posts, when green, were over 100 pounds, and it took some energy to put the top ones up.

Milton Swerdfeger,
Glen Stewart, Ontario

FACE TO FACE, NOSE TO NOSE

*L*aughter was very important in those days . . . sometimes it saved people's sanity during the Depression. My mother used to tell stories of those who could not laugh and shot themselves or drove into the Iroquois Canal when things got too rough.

She spent long hours behind the counter when Dad was away with the truck. She usually managed to lighten those hours by seeing the funny side of things. One incident which delighted her concerns two farmers who collided, one coming in, one going out of the store. We had a "stoop" built on to the store veranda in winter for protection from the northwest wind. George Irah Fader was coming through the stoop and John Fawcett was going out. Each man had been talking to someone behind him and each turned in time to collide, face to face, nose to nose.

Each backed off, shocked and insulted. Then, without a blessed word to one another, John Fawcett went out and George Irah Fader came in. Behind the counter, my mother was suffering from uncontrollable laughter and had to sally out to the storehouse, where only coal oil drums and boxes of puffed wheat would hear her. What was so funny to my mother was that it never occured to those two men to laugh about it.

Enid Swerdfeger,
Glen Stewart,
Ontario

SWAT FLIES

*M*y father-in-law was Arthur F. Choate. His father, Thomas, built the Warsaw store. Warsaw, Ontario is named for Warsaw, New York, because Thomas Choate learned his trade there. A cousin, Zaccheus Burnham, was to build a mill on the Indian River and he sent Thomas Choate to look after the mill, and he stayed. He built the store, too. But I think he was fonder of his singing classes than of the mill or store. He had his classes up over the store where we would live later.

It was a cold place to live, just the plaster on the inside and sheeting on the outside. We put beaver board over every room but the kitchen. The stove was in the basement under the store.

Grandma Choate and I didn't hit it off very well together. This day I was helping Evelyn Hawthorne clean up the store. We had been working hard and Evelyn and I both sat down. And you *never* sat down on a job in the store but what Grandma in the house knew it. And she came out with two fly-swatters. She said, "Here, if you must sit, swat flies!"

Beatrice Choate,
Warsaw, Ontario

MOOSE MEAT HAMBURGER

Our Pincher Creek store was a good living. We enjoyed it. We had 32 years of it here. I quit the meat-cutting part of it first. Meat-cutters got so damned expensive and so independent that I said, "O.K., I'll do the meat-cutting and get extra help in the grocery department." But I found meat-cutting a bit too heavy; I got health problems and had to quit it.

We would get an awful lot of game to process in the fall of the year. On the edge of Waterton Lakes National Park, of course, the hunting was good. A family could get enough game to carry them through the winter. A man could get a moose, an elk and a deer; in those days he was allowed one of each. That and a pork for some bacon and ham, and he'd got it whipped.

There was bear hunting done, too. I've never cared for it. A bear ham, cured and smoked, tastes just like pork. But a bear skinned out, looks exactly like a muscular man. There was a lot of poaching done, but we were under the authority of the Game Branch and we had to register everything that came in and it had to be proven by licence, so we didn't see too much of it.

But we would be down there some nights until midnight cutting game meat. Marion is short and she'd have to stand on a butter box to put the meat through the hamburger machine.

"I'd stand there for hours making moose meat hamburger 'til I looked like it. Then I had to package it all. The two-pound packages weren't too bad, but when people wanted one-pound packages, that took forever."

John and Marion Green,
Pincher Creek, Alberta

SERVING THE AMERICAN BASE AT ARGENTIA

*T*he people from the base came here to cash their cheques. Muriel Palfrey was nearly a bank. She had the money ready for them and whatever change was on their cheques . . . 50¢ or 75¢ or 99¢ . . .they would give it to her. Maybe she would cash 30 cheques in a day.

If you came in and asked for something special, she would say, "I haven't got it now but I'll get it by tomorrow evening." She would phone St. John's and have it sent by taxi. There was always a taxi going back and forth to the base so they would charge a dollar or two to bring out a package: a scythe to mow hay; or an awl to sew leather; heels for your shoes; an emanel-covered pail; a washboard.

Muriel used to be open until one or two o'clock, sometimes three o'clock, in the morning, because they would come from the base that late. There was one beer tavern and they would stop on the way home and get canned sausage and bread and cheese. Or the girls would come when they'd get their cheques and buy shoes and dresses and all, late at night. It was the only place around you could get a dress. She'd get hundreds of dollars from each girl.

She could sleep for an hour and get up and go on. Next day she would be adding up bills or putting prices on tinned soup and everything would stop and she'd be sound asleep. Five minutes would do her. Then she'd be fresh; she's a very relaxed person. She always says, "I love everything I do in the store.

"I could stay in it seven days a week. The only thing I hate is housework. I love meeting people. I find everybody nice."

Maureen Linehan,
Placentia, Newfoundland

FELL SOME TREES AND BUILD A STORE

*T*he next two falls, 1928 and 1929, I'd be sent off to run an outpost at Pickerel Narrows on Granville Lake, 75 or more miles to the northeast of Pukatawagan (in Northern Manitoba), spending from September to May there. The place consisted of 15 or so Indian families and we travelled out of there by dogs to buy fur on a straight barter basis.

I was given an Indian helper who would live with me, and I was sent off with him along with 12 dogs and a flotilla of six or more canoes loaded with trade goods for the store. We had to paddle, as the post had only one 2 $^{1}/_{2}$-horsepower engine, for main post use only. We would take six dogs to a canoe, plus whatever else it would take. We found out, whenever we got to shore, that the dogs all wanted to get out at the same time on the same side of the canoe.

My boss told me that, when I got to Pickerel Narrows, I would have to fell some trees and build a store. Also, the cabin I would use, might be in disrepair. This proved to be the case. It had a dirt roof with daylight showing, a broken-down door, a floor of sorts; and the logs would have to be rechinked with moss. For a mattress I would find a nearby hay meadow and could use hay and a canvas to make one.

The store was duly built with the logs of the forest. Counter shelves and floor were constructed of axe-hewn poles. For the store roof I had rubberoid roofing, but none for the log shack.

Each fall we had to net five to six thousand white fish for winter dog feed. They were stored in a log cache on sticks of 12, which were then placed on horizontal poles. The fall weather dried them out enough to preserve them for the winter.

As soon as the ice was strong enough, we set out to periodically visit the scattered trappers' camps to buy their fur. It was straight barter . . . no cash involved . . . and we could take about 700 pounds of mixed merchandise on the two toboggans.

Ralph Butchart,
Pickerel Narrows, Manitoba

SAWED OFF

*M*other made ice cream in the summertime and sold it on Saturday night. There was no other place to go, so they all came to the store on Saturday night. She would make several freezers full, then pack it in ice.

We had our own ice, used to bring it in every winter. We'd have a good crew on and every year some fellow would be cutting with a cross-cut saw and saw himself into the water.

You see, they'd make a cut 12 or 15 feet one way, then they'd start cutting across the other way in 2-foot pieces. Some fellow would be standing on a 2-foot cake and he'd saw it off.

Edward Stoddard,
Port Clyde, Nova Scotia

This was the W.W. McClelland store in Niagara-on-the-Lake, Ontario as it looked in its busy early days.

OUR HOLIDAY

We have worked hard, but not like my father worked. In summertime, he would close the store after six o'clock and go kill a pig or calf in the evening. He did a lot of trading during the Depression: calves, cows, lambs, pigs. So he would kill a pig every week, and kill the lambs also to sell the meat in the store. And three or four mornings a week he would get up at five o'clock to skin the calves and cows. A man came from Montreal every two weeks for the hides; that was a good market . . . $1 for a hide, calf or cow.

In winter, he got up at four o'clock and did a load of wood before eight o'clock, and he worked in the store until five o'clock, then he made one more load of wood and he's getting back about nine or ten o'clock in the evening. He had to go to the farmer and get the wood, load the wood and bring it here, and next day deliver it to the people who had ordered it.

Last fall, I was with my brother where they built the Hydro-Quebec station, where they spent about 55 million dollars. As I stood there, I told my brother that I remember in 1939 when the King and Queen came to Montreal in May, all the stores in Quebec were closed. That day I come here with my father to pile the wood in cords. That was our holiday.

Guy Richer,
St. Jovite, Quebec

SHE FELL SO NICE

I came here for a month and I hated storekeeping. I had been working in a bank. Every day I hated it worse. But it got busy for Christmas and I said I would stay until after Christmas. Then there was stock-taking, I stayed for that. Then I was hooked. I've been here for twenty-five years.

And we had our fun. We girls didn't just work here and leave work and never see each other again. We'd all go off together to a dance, and have fried chicken at my place after.

We had our fun in the store too. We were emptying this great big cardboard box and we put Cecily in it when the carpenters were building this part on. So we called in Mr. Barns. ''Mr. Barns, would you come and help me move this?''

"Yes, me darlin', I will."

"Now don't hurt yourself."

"No." So he tried and tried and up popped Cecily! We were always playing tricks.

And the customers! There were two ladies, one was about 200 pounds and she used to hum all the time. And this friend of hers was as thin as could be. So she was hummin' this day, "Hum . . . Hum . . . De . . . Dum," and she fell over a sack of onions. She fell just like a feather, she fell so nice. And here was this thin woman trying to pick up this 200-pound friend. Well, if she was *killed*, I couldn't have helped her. Cecily and I and Muriel thought we'd die laughing. She fell like a feather, didn't she?

Maureen Linehan,
Placentia, Newfoundland

LAUGH ABOUT IT LATER

I was a "detail salesman" for Quaker Oats after the war in the Peterborough-Lindsay area of Ontario. I would go into the store and take orders, "detail orders", nothing but Quaker products. I would take these orders to the wholesaler and say, "I've sold 200 cases of rolled oats so that will take your stock down to 50 cases, so you should order 500." If we did a good job, we could really influence sales in our district. Of course, the Robin Hood man would be out there doing the same thing. We'd meet on the road all the time and we were very good friends, but we were deadly competitors, too. He was a good salesman, so was I.

You'd go in . . . you had to be very polite. First thing you'd say, "Do you mind if I check the shelves first?" You'd check the pricing, and if it was dusty, you'd dust it off and you'd line it up on the shelf and try to expand your facing on the shelf. If the storekeeper had a damaged package, you'd buy it back at his selling price. Then if you could enter his "holy ground" . . . basement or warehouse . . . you'd check the back stock. You'd quickly count it all up, check the dates and change it around so he would use up the older stuff first.

I was up in Minden where Sam Welch ran an old-fashioned store. He had shelves right up to a 12- or 15-foot ceiling. I got

Wooden bins behind the counter contained brown sugar and rolled oats that had to be scooped out and bagged when the customer wanted a pound or two. This store is at Val Gagné in Northern Ontario.

79

up on a high stool where he had some packages of Aunt Jemima Pancake Flour sitting on the top shelf. I had to get these down, because the damn things had dust on the top and they were old. So I'm on top of the stool reaching up to the flour and the stool shattered and I went down . . . the stool was so old, completely brittle, dried out. Coming down, I clawed the cigarette shelf right below the flour, and I got showered with cigarette packages and cigars. I was sitting there on the floor and this package of Aunt Jemima tumbled off and whacked me on the head.

Boy! Old Sam was pretty mad . . . blamed me. He insisted I pay for the stool. And he made me restock the shelf.

He was pretty upset at the time. But afterwards, when I'd come in, the two of us would have a good laugh about it.

Ken Gadd,
Peterborough, Ontario

BREAKING AWAY

I can remember having 15 or 18 people in here, some until 12 o'clock at night. Rose Valley people worked 'til sundown and then they came to the store. There was an old gentleman down the road who would get two jugs of molasses, then with a bag of groceries on his shoulder and carrying these two gallons of molasses, he would walk two and a half miles home. Probably after following the horses all day, harrowing.

When we started closing on Wednesday afternoons, at first we just had to pull the blinds, get in the rig and go. If you didn't, there would be two coming down and three coming up. And a lot of them were . . . well, belligerent is not quite the right word . . . but it was, "The very idea! You better stay here. We need stuff."

Ben Cousins,
Rose Valley, Prince Edward Island

CHAPTER SIX

MOVING THE GOODS

The male Canadian storekeeper has traditionally not been one to stay indoors behind the counter. On any given day, you would be more likely to find his female counterpart working behind the counter (as well as running the household) while he was out there moving the goods. On some days this would mean cutting . . . or at least carting . . . the wood, which he would pile out behind the store and truck away through the winter as customers needed it. On other days he would be unloading carloads of gluten or bran or shorts at the station, and trucking it home where it had to be unloaded into his feedshed, whence it would be carried out again to a farmer's wagon or truck. Ben Cousins of Rose Valley, Prince Edward Island might be off trucking his farmers' hogs to market. Myrs Tretiak of Broad Valley, Manitoba might be making his regular 80-mile trip to Winnipeg to haul back groceries, oil, grease and auto parts in his van. A very large part of a storekeeper's time has always been spent in moving the goods.

In some establishments, the storekeeper or his staff actually delivered the goods to the customer's door. This might be a formal route, as in McNaughton's of Moosomin, Saskatchewan. Or it might be very informal, a farmer's wife ringing up the store, "Joe's busy in the field and I need pickling salt. Can you run it out to me?"

Over the past century, the railway has played a dominant role in getting the goods to the store. Before the railway, there were ox teams and canoe brigades. There were three-day trips with a wagon across the Qu'Appelle Valley and back, in the early 1900s. As late as the 1940s, there were teams and sleighs carting food and bags of feed to stores across Canada when wild winter storms blocked the roads.

And always the goods, which had to be lifted, toted, shifted, stacked and restacked, were heavy: drums of coal oil, tons of coal, bags of bran, rolls of linoleum, crates of oranges; and awkward: sides of pork or beef, stalks of bananas, live turkeys, breakable eggs, enormous bags of seneca roots. If a Canadian storekeeper was not born strong, he either became strong or expired trying to move the goods. Small storekeepers like Milton Swerdfeger, who weighed 116 pounds, learned to handle bags of bran weighing 112 pounds. At the opposite end of the scale was Daniel MacDonald, a storekeeper in Lindsay, Ontario, known as the Lindsay strongman. His epitaph reads:

Ye weak beware! Here lyes the strong,
A victim to his strength,
He lifted Sixteen Hundred pounds,
And here he lays at length.

As early trucks replaced horses and wagons, they speeded up the business of getting goods to the country store. This Fargo truck carted gluten, bran, shorts and middlings, loads of coal, cement, shingles and cedar posts to the Glen Stewart store.

BY DOG SLED

Both years at Pickerel Narrows we would be short of supplies before Christmas, so that January through March was taken up by bringing merchandise from Pukatawagan. The round trip would be about 150 miles. Going in light, provided there was a bit of a trail, we took two days. We had poor dogs and were never able to ride, so it meant long hours of trotting behind them. The trip back with a load took three days with one night sleeping out in the bush. If the trails were bad with heavy snow, it might mean two nights outside. One night would always be spent at an Indian encampment at High Rock in a family shack. High Rock was the midway point between Pickerel Narrows and Pukatawagan.

This type of life was arduous and demanding, but a person got a great deal of satisfaction in meeting the challenge and being equal to the rigours of portaging, running rapids, paddling and dog sledding. It seemed to be the accepted thing to live off the country and not be too dependent on basic foods. Each spring we would be out of groceries by season's end and one year, for the four-day trip back to Pukatawagan, we lived on boiled sturgeon.

Ralph Butchart,
Lac du Bonnet, Manitoba

PACK HORSES ON THE FRASER

You must remember our Pavilion store supplied everybody for 20 miles or so. And the people on the other side of the Fraser River used to come in with a string of pack horses. They used to buy sugar by the sack, milk by the case, rice even by the sack. Flour, of course, always by the 100-pound sack. They'd swim their horses across the river. There's no bridge today, there never was a bridge.

When I arrived in Pavilion in the late 1940s, they had a rowboat there with an operator, and that was our ferry. And a horse trail went down there. Tony Montgomery, he was the ferry operator and he lived down there. The Montgomerys owned a ranch on the other side of the river. This Tony Montgomery, he had an artifical leg, but he was like a mountain goat, the muscles just bulging on him from rowing. He was tough, very tough.

If it was going to be a lot of stuff, they'd have to bring pack horses over. So they'd have ropes to tie them to the boat and they'd whack the horses and the boat would start pushing out and the horses would follow it. Remember, these horses got used to it after a while and they knew.

When they were going across . . . the current is very strong there, very strong . . . so what they did, they're going from A to B, they'd go upstream in the back eddies, quite a distance, something like maybe 150 yards and then start pulling out. And they always pointed the boat upstream and the current just brought them down, and by the time they landed they were over here, opposite.

Then in the wintertime, a lot of packing was done. Feed for horses, sacks of oats, seed for planting were taken across. They used what they called an ice bridge, which was really a jam of ice floes. The ice would be solid but all jagged with the water flowing underneath. There was a fellow called Joe Fletcher who lost a horse and saddle through the ice . . . the horse went through.

In the old days, when they had the flour mill at Pavilion store, there used to be packers who would take the goods all the way up to Barkerville. That was in the gold rush. They used the ice bridges.

John Moss,
Pavilion, British Columbia

BY PLANE

*A*fter 12 months at Gogama, I was given the store at Red Lake, Ontario to manage. We arrived by the last plane of the winter. The spring was protracted and cold, and the area was looking forward to the first barges coming in from Hudson Bay with fresh supplies. Meat was scarce, but the planes were asked to fly in and drop sacks of it on the ice, which was too weak for landing. The dogs became aware of this as some of the packages split on impact, so when a plane was heard, they were first out on the ice.

Ralph Butchart,
Red Lake, Ontario

TRIPS TO GIROUX

My father, John W. Reimer, had a farm adjacent to the village, but he also was a teamster, hauling from Winnipeg to the Reimer stores. Oxen were used here up to 1920, although I never drove them myself. They were better in the mud . . . their feet spread out. I have got stuck with horses in the mud, and they couldn't get themselves out. And all the trouble to hitch another horse to them to get them pulled out! Oxen would very seldom get into the mud so they couldn't get out. In the early days it sometimes took from Monday to Friday to get to Winnipeg and back . . . sure, oxen were slow.

I went with Father on trips to Winnipeg when I was very young, each of us driving a team. We stayed in Winnipeg, and there were stopping houses in between. I remember we had a load of seneca roots, bags eight feet high and three feet in diameter and they were laid across the wagon box. So I was three feet high above the double wagon box and that's where I sat. I remember paying toll at the bridge, I've forgotten whether it was the Red River or the Assiniboine.

Seneca roots was a cash crop which the settlers could sell in the store; it was used as a kind of medicine. The area had miles and miles of the wild plants, you could just dig them out.

One of Klaas Reimer's sons, Klaas W. Reimer, went to Winnipeg to learn cheese-making in the early, early days when you sometimes had to walk to Winnipeg to get what you wanted. But he got it; he saw the need. He won first prize for cheese in 1897 at the Toronto Exhibition, and a gold medal at the Pan American Exhibition in the United States in 1901. So that was one product that they could finish and sell . . . the cheese.

Butter was another one. I do remember the butter tubs very well. I handled hundreds, maybe thousands of them hauling freight to and from Giroux after the railway reached Giroux. My father did that for 20 years, and I had my share of it.

I remember trips to Giroux when it was so bad. We had a sleigh with a wide platform so it would be easier to load . . . barrels of syrup, kerosene and such that weighed 300 to 400 pounds. When I was about 13 I'd go all by myself to Giroux. There were people there who would help; my uncle lived there. It was probably about 1910, in the later part of the afternoon, when a storm came up, a real heavy storm. And I had to go past bush along the road and that had filled up with drifts. I went in there and it was so hard for the horses, they had to jump to get out of the snow. It got too heavy, they couldn't pull that wide sleigh anymore. I had to give it up.

I unhitched and went home. It was a good two miles from Steinbach. I remember I had rubber boots and some sheepskin shoes inside those, but above that there was only one pair of stockings and, riding on the horses, the pants lifted up and there was the almost bare leg, and the wind from the north was very cold.

In those days it was different than it is now. When you came back the next day, the stuff was all there.

John C. Reimer,
Steinbach, Manitoba

STUNT MAN

*W*hen I was still at home on the farm, we would draw loads for the stores which sold feed and coal. One nice fall day old Mr. Coulthart asked me to go to Embrun for a load of coal. We had very lively horses; only one could be driven with a slack line. I took this one and a very high-spirited, four-year-old black. I drove into the town to the carload of coal and got the wagon loaded. As we were leaving, a train blew for a crossing. This black horse turned her head into the other horse and when she turned back, the snap on the inside line came unfastened from the ring on the bit in her mouth.

Now I couldn't control the team, as the black had only one line on the outside and this pulled her to the side of the road. In no time they were running on the paved road. I tried every way to stop them but couldn't, as I was pulling them toward the ditch.

The wagon was new and I noticed the whiffletrees were out past the wheel. The weight of the load kept the tugs tight, so I watched for the proper place on the road so as not to stumble. I handed John Coulthart the lines and told him to hold them just so. When I came to the right spot, I jumped from the front of the wagon just outside the front wheel. I caught the tug which was tight from pulling the load. Two or three strides took me to the back pad; then I caught the hame stick which was up past the collar. I knew then I was safe.

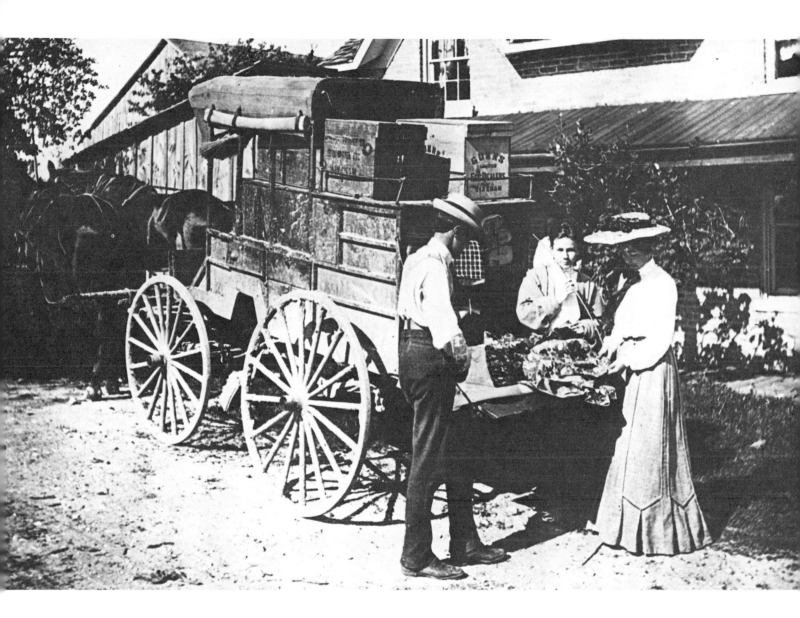

I jerked the line on the big horse. He threw up his head and slowed a little, which let the black come around toward me. I caught the ring of her bit and jerked them to a stop. When I finally got a look at Mr. Coulthart, he was as white as paper. When I got back on the wagon, I realized it was a risky thing to do but I could see no other way to stop the team.

Milton Swerdfeger,
Morewood, Ontario

Early merchants often took the goods to the customer. Peddlers were a common sight on country roads, and a welcome diversion for womenfolk who rarely got away to town.

DON'T BE FOOLISH

*I*n wintertime, P.E.I roads would be closed, sometimes from November to April. One year they closed on the last day of October. I remember, because I was caught out with the truck hauling feed. Didn't get home until the middle of the night.

I got a horse in Crapaud to get home. I went to one particular party and the best he would do was put us up for the night. No way would he volunteer to take me home or give me a horse. There were two fellows with me and they were down in the dumps like I was. I said, "We're not through yet. We'll have a mile to walk to this place, but I feel *quite* sure we'll get a horse."

So we landed in there and he said, "Ben, there's only one horse in the barn that would take you home tonight and I have a sick cow . . . I don't know what to say.

"No," he says, "you can take the horse! I have an old mare here. I can go across the field to my father's place on her back and get a horse there if I need to go for a vet." So he gave me the horse and a sleigh.

And only it was a good horse, I don't think we could have got home. There were snow drifts four or five feet deep. Up around Rose Valley corner, it was hard to see where we were going and the horse missed the road and dropped into the ditch. We could just see the top of her head. But she was a good horse; we jumped off the sleigh and she got back up on the road.

And not a nickel charged when I took it back and offered to pay him. "Don't be foolish," he says.

Ben Cousins,
Rose Valley, Prince Edward Island

HAULING FROM HARTLAND

*D*ad used to go to Woodstock for the grocery stock, leave early in the morning because that was a 20-mile round trip, a long way for the horses. But I would take the horses over the covered bridge into Hartland for drugs and other things.

I remember when we used to go over the covered bridge in winter, a lot of farmers would be hauling grain over, and they would have to snow the bridge. They would haul in snow and make a track for the horses and sleighs to go on. It was a $20 fine if you ran your horses on the covered bridge.

The western spans of the bridge went out once with the ice, back in 1920. Mother remembers because that was the night Muriel was born. Dr. McIntosh had to walk the planks to get across.

Lloyd DeWare,
Waterville, New Brunswick

HORSES, SHIRTS AND HATS

Once I took three carloads of horses to Montreal to be used in snow removal. I bought bankrupt stock and brought it back: shirts 70¢, hats 75¢. We sold all but three hats. One night years later when it was raining, I was cleaning out under the counter. Three guys came in half-drunk, going to a party in a boxcar at Mississippi. "What regalia have you got?"

"Haven't got anything."

"Come on. What you got that we can wear?"

So I got the three hats out and sold them for $1.75 apiece.

Walter Cameron,
Fallbrook, Ontario

WILD RICE

Taylor had a big store . . . the Keene Emporium . . . and he dealt in wild rice from 1919 to 1949. He had a spring house behind the old grist mill, and they put the rice right into the water and kept it there in the springtime. Then Taylor packed it and sent it out by train. He bought it from the Indians, not parched for eating, but with the hull on, for planting.

They put the rice in wooden boxes lined with moss, then some ice, then moss on the top. And shipped it that way. Taylor's Seed Rice went to five outlets in England and to the Rhine, to Austria, Switzerland and Brazil. Taylor went to different places and planted it himself for people.

Phil Beattie,
Keene, Ontario

TOMBSTONES

Oh yes, he had everything. He could get you a tombstone. He went out one time with a machinery agent to the country to sell a machine and they come to this woman's place. She said, "What all do you sell?"

He said, "Oh, I've got everything, up to tombstones."

"Tombstones!" she said. "I want one!" They had had a child dead for quite a long time and they wanted a tombstone.

He set up his own tombstone. Mother died first. And there would be little headstones to put up later. Not many people do set up their own tombstone.

Barbara (Schram) Mattis,
Richdale, Alberta

HORSE DELIVERY

McNaughton's of Moosomin maintained the horse delivery right to the end. The old horse would sometimes choose the most inopportune times to run away. Upset all the groceries. That was typical. No matter how placid the horse was, once in a while he would get giddy and have to have a run. He'd probably run for three or four blocks and then stop and look as though he'd never done anything wrong in his life.

They did try a truck for a while but it wasn't satisfactory. The old horse knew its way around much better. And McNaughton's did give unbelievable delivery service. Unbelievable in today's world. You could have a spool of thread delivered in the morning and, if you ran out of that colour, you could have another one in the afternoon.

But don't forget, every other store in town had a horse-drawn delivery too, back in the '30s. The delivery man was busy from morning to night. He hauled from the station, too, so he would mostly be busy in the morning hauling in, and in the afternoon, hauling out. They had a tarp to throw over when it rained.

Every household in town knew the delivery man's horse. One of the councillors was running for office and he thought he'd put a campaign on. So he put "Vote for Pennington" and a picture on each side of every delivery horse in town. There were probably six horses. So for eight or nine days every horse in town wore his picture, house to house.

Bert McKay,
Moosomin, Saskatchewan

ICE

When you delivered ice to a customer, the block was always too small. We would deliver the ice from eight o'clock to nine-thirty in the morning, and ten-thirty someone would phone my father, "Hey, your son came and delivered the ice and gave me only a small block." Of course they had left it sitting outside in the hot weather.

In summer, we would go every day to Lac Maskinonge and Lac Duhamel to deliver the groceries and the ice. We would get up at five o'clock to prepare the orders and we were leaving about eight o'clock. At first we delivered with a horse and wagon, then with a car. After 1946 we had a truck.

In May and June and from September to the 15th of October, we delivered ice every other day. But in July and August, every day. It was a membership, they paid $5 for the whole season, from May to October 15. When we stopped it in 1947, it had gone up to $10.

Guy Richer,
St. Jovite, Quebec

FOUR AND TWENTY CROWS

Working in our store on the Curve Lake Reserve, I just automatically became bilingual. My parents mostly talked English but everybody who came to the store before the advent of radio talked Indian (Ojibway). When the pre-school kids came up to the store, they all talked Indian. You just wound up with two words for everything.

I bought furs for years. In later days, I used to go out and buy furs, but in my father's day, they used to bring them into the store. I grew up with furs. I used to go trapping with my father.

In the spring of the year when they couldn't get around by the road into the reserve and the ferry couldn't get across, they used to paddle the bread across the lake with canoes. They would bring the bread out by truck to the Selwyn side and then paddle it across. Bread wasn't wrapped in those days. It came in double loaves, and we wrapped it on Friday night using newspaper. And the print didn't come off in those days.

But this lad bringing the bread across, upset the canoe. The lad didn't drown. But all I remember was the loaves of bread floating. When I went out with my father to go trapping, bread was floating around all over the lake. And the crows were sitting on these loaves of bread.

Cliff Whetung,
Curve Lake, Ontario

MOVING THE FISH

*I*n the spring, we merchants went in to St. John's and brought down the supplies for the summer, including a shipload of salt. We got this on credit, all in good faith, hoping for a good fishery. Then we supplied the fishermen on credit, so when their fish was hard cured (sun dried), it was graded and shipped accordingly. They were paid at a price agreed upon by the fish trade. The bigger buyers in St. John's knew the market and they came up with a suggested price and that price was credited to the fisherman's account.

In the fall, the fish would be packed for export to various markets, some in four-quintal casks and eventually in smaller casks. Also, in the fall, we would get in a six-month's supply of food, flour, sugar, biscuits, everything in bulk. When the fisherman came to straighten up after his fish was shipped, he paid what he owed from the summer and perhaps a bit of what he owed before if he had a bad year before. Then he would take his winter supply home by horse and dray, or motorboat or dog team.

To hard cure the fish they would leave it in salt five or six days, then they would wash it and spread it out on the flakes to dry. If they let it stay out in the hot sun, instead of gradually drying the fish, the hot sun would scald it. That fish would be bad when it was cooked.

Culling the fish was our most unthankful job. The fisherman wouldn't always agree with you if his fish was sunburned or got too much heat. There was a fish inspector who would inspect it when it was being packed for market, but we had to cull it first on the wharf.

If you were in business here you had to have a wharf in conjunction with your store. Your wharf was your road. The fisherman brought his fish by boat from his stage (wharf) to yours. The fish came up the wharf on a trolley on a track; the provisions went down that way to his boat.

We would pack the fish in barrels. It used to go in 4-quintal barrels which was 448 pounds. Then in 200-pound barrels. Then 128. Then 64.

Some of our markets took fish in bulk. Mostly the Portuguese. A ship would come and be here for days. We would carry the fish out of our big fish store in hand bars, load it into motorboats and take it out, and it would be yaffled off the motorboats into the ship.

Bill Ashbourne and Herb Gillett,
Twillingate, Newfoundland

Country stores are "merchants in everything". At this popular Cold Springs, Ontario store, goods spill outside onto veranda, roadside and lawn.

CHAPTER SEVEN

SURVIVAL IN THE THIRTIES

In general, rural people fared better than their contemporaries in town during the Depression. The close-knit little community stretched its pockets and tightened its belt and made some way to help those in need. Usually it was

Even oxen were pressed into duty to serve instead of gasoline . . . a cold, slow trip to the store in north-central Alberta.

the storekeeper who directly cushioned the shock and carried the debt.

If people in his community were starving, he was expected to feed them, or go down in local history as the merchant who "refused" them. There are stories in every community about what the storekeeper did when the customer's chips were down. One New Brunswick woman remembers a neighbour coming to their farmhouse door with tears in his eyes because the storekeeper had "turned him down". The country creed of sharing what you had almost demanded that a merchant give goods free when someone was down and out. Of course, there was the everlasting chance that you might be paid some day. Storekeepers who knew their customers, knew just how remote those chances were in some cases.

There are heart-warming stories, too, of young families starting out in the worst of all possible times, carried through the 1930s by the local storekeeper. "Maurice St. Laurent was full of a good heart. Those first years on my farm, I bought my seed in the spring and paid him in the fall. 'Give me your note. Pay me next fall.' " Joe Denis remembers what a help that was.

A woman in Alberta remembers getting a shiny new kitchen range from George Schram when she was newly married and had no money; and how she paid him in little bits saved from her milk money.

The ingenuity of storekeepers in the 1930s is remarkable. In finding ways to get themselves paid, they almost got water from a stone. At Glen Stewart, Milton Swerdfeger took cows on account and rented them back to the farmer on a share arrangement that gave him the first calf. Other storekeepers dealt in blueberries, mica, wild rice, cowhides, even gopher tails, anything at all that could be carted or shipped somewhere and turned into that rare commodity . . . cash.

Not all storekeepers survived. In western Canada, some of them watched the farmers desert their drought-stricken farms, and knew they had to leave also. "Going broke, going insolvent, failing, going under, going bankrupt" were expressions that were all too common. Only the tough, the competent and the lucky ones would hold on until it was over.

STRUGGLING TO KEEP THEIR SANITY

*P*ersonally, we did not suffer during this period. Our suffering was in watching our customers struggling to keep their sanity, shipping stock to the market, receiving nothing but a bill for the shipping charges; wells going dry, necessitating a drive of 10 miles each day for water for their dwindling stock; seeding optimistically each spring, only to have the seed blown out; lack of moisture year after year, until the earth felt like a ball of powder in which the ever-rolling, tumbling Russian thistle spread around; dust penetrating everywhere; finally, and for the last straw, the invasion of the grasshopper just when a small crop was in sight, killing hopes for yet another year.

It was an uncomfortable period to live through. The relief orders, first issued by the municipalities and then by the Federal government, provided the customers with a means of purchasing groceries and clothing from us and kept our credit good. When the municipality went broke, we were left holding the bag for a number of years, but did receive payment when it was solvent, which was like found gold.

We ourselves ate as well as ever, dressed as well, drove a relatively new car and suffered not at all. We helped distribute carloads of vegetables and clothing shipped to us from the East. I was secretary-treasurer of the Relief Committee. We held dances and raised money for relief purposes. We made several trips to Regina for clothing brought in through the church from more affluent areas, to the drought-stricken congregations of the West. We canvassed the district for the needy's requirements and tried to give help where the need was most urgent.

To some of our customers who had practised frugality and economy all their lives, this was just another challenge. They used their relief orders for flour, yeast, sugar, dried fruit, dried vegetables and the basics, and lived with proper nourishment. It was the untaught who suffered, the ones who bought loaves of bread, canned vegetables and fruit, the finished product, lived well for a week, and practically starved for three. It is this latter group which is indebted to us today. Their relief order never covered their wants.

In 1934, we left the Worcester district where Russian thistle, the dust and the grasshoppers still dominated the scene, and moved further north and returned to the grain-buying business. In our six years in merchandising, we had learned so much about our fellow men . . . the courage of so many of them who faced that dark period in their lives, hit an all-time low but bounced back, and today they have almost forgotten the era existed.

I don't think they will ever forget though, when one pail of water had to bath the baby, wash his clothes, wash off the kitchen floor and, finally, water the garden.

Mr. and Mrs. John Ringstrom,
Worcester, Saskatchewan

SMALL THINGS

*M*other operated the store for about 25 years. In the '30s she operated a little differently than most stores. She used to say, "If you do three small things, it makes a big thing." She would sell a quarter pound of tea. Or she would buy a dozen eggs for 8¢ and sell them for 10¢. She would sell somebody a half pound of lard if that was what they wanted. She also sold butter papers so people who made butter could wrap it and she could sell it in Shelburne.

A lot of people would run up big bills at the stores because their husbands would go away and work for the summer. But if a husband got hurt and couldn't work . . . ? Mother's customers never ran big bills. They'd send her six eggs and want six eggs' worth of tea. That's the kind of business she did. "Three small things makes a big thing."

Joseph Ross,
Cape Negro, Nova Scotia

NO OUTHOUSE AT ALL

I worked in Dad's store and I trained to be a school teacher. Schools were scarce in 1933 and 1934. I went out to one place, and of course you had to board in the community. Well, I had to stay at school until dark because there were no bathroom facilities at all at the house.

I remember the first night I came and, oh, everything smelled so good . . . the bread was cooking. And I thought I had a good place. (Although the kids had impetigo and that didn't look too good.) Anyway, I said to the lady of the house, "You know, I really have to go to the bathroom."

She said, "Oh, my daughter will take you."

So we set out and we kept going and going, and she said, "Anytime now."

And I didn't know what she meant. Prairie, a little bit of brush . . . and we were away past the barn. I thought this biffie must be away far out somewhere. She said again, "Anytime now."

Finally she said, "I'm going to do it right here." And then I caught on.

I phoned Dad on the party line that I wanted to come home and he said, "Stella, just stay one more week."

I said, "Dad, I can't explain but I have to come home." The school kids were nice, I hated to leave. But I just couldn't stand it.

So I came back to the store and helped Dad until I was given a chance of teaching in our own town. But my mother was very disappointed in me. She thought I should have stayed. When I came home and explained, she said, "Stella, there are worse things than that!"

Saskatchewan

SCURVY

*I*n the spring of 1929 at Pukatawagan, the Indians told us about two white trappers who were living in a tent 25 miles away, very sick, down with what we found to be scurvy. One of them was totally immobilized and the other could only crawl from the tent to the lake edge to get water. We knew these men as they had arrived at the post the previous fall to get away from the outside "depression". They had built a cabin, killed a moose or two, lived on a scanty diet devoid of vegetables and fell ill of scurvy when spring came.

Solomon and I set out on the rotting ice with a sleigh and canoe to rescue them. We would travel on good ice on foot, pulling the sleigh and canoe, then transfer to the canoe when open water occurred.

They were in very bad shape, with sore backs and joints, flesh like putty, loose teeth and smelling somewhat. We took a crossbar out of the canoe, made a stretcher out of poles and canvas, and levered the sicker man into the canoe and the other recumbent alongside his partner. Three or four days later we delivered them to Pukatawagan over four portages round the various falls of the Churchill River. Subsequently, they were sent to a hospital at Island Falls . . . the hydro plant for the new town of Flin Flon. They made a good recovery.

Ralph Butchart,
Pukatawagan, Manitoba

IT KILLED HIM

*T*he farmers were really better off in the 1920s than they are today. But when the '30s came, everything crashed. We had one farmer who was a very fine man; he always had a lot of hogs and he would ship hogs with us. He had 10 or 12 just ready to ship. And then the slump . . . we couldn't get him 4¢ a pound.

Well, he butchered and barrelled some of them, and probably shipped some to the soap factory in Charlottetown. But it killed him really. He was just that kind. He was about 45 and he died of a heart attack.

Katie MacLeod,
Vernon River, Prince Edward Island

TWO WOMEN

*W*e bought the McArthur's Mills store in 1933, in the middle of the Depression. We cashed cheques for the whole area, driving 18 miles to the bank every week.

Money was scarce in 1933. Men received 88¢ per day working on the road. I knew two women who followed the road grader . . . throwing off stones . . . in order to help with the finances.

But we got to know and trust everyone. When a man said he would pay on Friday . . . Friday it was . . . or he came to explain.

Marjorie Slater,
McArthur's Mills, Ontario

CARLOADS OF FOOD TO SASKATCHEWAN

*W*hen Saskatchewan had crop failures in the 1930s, we sent carloads of food from here . . . somebody sent pumpkins, I remember that well. Pumpkins! But people were really good about it. Tom La Brick, he had a potato bin in his basement and he took me down there. "What I've got to decide is to keep enough for the family and for seed, and the rest can go." He had three 90-pound bags to send.

Charlie Chamberlin,
Wakefield, Quebec

This is July 1934. Mr. P. Ashley Cooper, Governor of the Hudson's Bay Company, and Mrs. Cooper are distributing gifts outside the Hudson's Bay store at Port Burwell.

NOTHING TO EAT

*J*ack Adams had an apartment of sorts over the blacksmith shop. One day the merchant from Hexton moved a family into it. They didn't have anything, not even to eat. I dug a pail of potatoes and gave them to the father. I told him to dig a row later. He was so lazy he didn't dig any.

Every weekend we filled a box of groceries to feed those kids. Later, Jack put them out. Just as the Hexton merchant moved them in, so I was glad to move them out, so some other storekeeper would have to feed them.

Milton Swerdfeger,
Glen Stewart, Ontario

MANNA FROM HEAVEN

*A*s a kid I used to read in the Bible about "manna from heaven". I'd say, "Well, I'd like to believe that, but that's too hard to believe."

My mother died in March of 1935 and things were very, very blue. I knew then that my father had cancer, too. I had a brother and two sisters and I was out of work . . . this was during the height of the Depression.

It was a day with wet snow in November, a very, very depressing day. And I felt very, very blue. It was the worst day I spent in my life . . . in spirit. The Salvation Army man came along . . . did I want to buy their newspaper, *The War Cry*?

I said, "Sir, I haven't got a dime. I have nothing."

He said, "If you promise to read it, I'll *give* it to you."

I said, "I will." In it there was a little poem, "Among the Black Clouds There's Always a Silver Lining". I read that and my spirit began to come back a little bit. From then on things worked out a little better.

Shortly after, I got up one morning and I looked out the back window. There was an open space we used as a ball field, and all I could see was partridge . . . prairie chickens. There had been a snowstorm that drove them down from the West. Those prairie chickens stayed there from November until the end of April. They were never there before and they have never been there since. Anybody that had a .22 that winter, had food. They were all over the country. That to me was the "manna from heaven".

Because we didn't have farms at Cheminis, we didn't have hogs or beef or eggs or whatever. That part of the country was very poor, because it was a boom town area and then all the work disappeared at once. Still today, when I meet my sister, she asks me if I remember the Day of the Prairie Chickens.

Albert Emond,
Cheminis, Ontario

PROSPERITY BONDS

Dave Bradshaw was loaded up in the store with these Prosperity Bonds. And I told him he should know better. Prosperity Bonds were born out of Social Credit. Aberhart was going to make his own currency. His theory was, the more money you print, the more purchasing power you had, but there was nothing behind these bonds, only the faith that people had in them. And that faith was only temporary.

A Prosperity Bond had the Seal of Alberta on the front of it and the back had 100 square patches and you bought these stamps. As long as you held a bond you were supposed to buy these 1¢ stamps and put one on for every day of the week in every one of these squares. I'm darned if I know where we bought the stamps. When you got a hundred on, you could send it and get it redeemed and get your money back. But the idea was to keep it moving, keep it hot so you wouldn't have to put a stamp on. The whole thing was to get money moving. If you voted Social Credit and followed Aberhart's theory, then you did that.

I was never Social Credit. No, I never was that crazy.

If you were dedicated to the cause, you accepted the bonds as legal tender within the province. But then it got so nobody wanted them, the wholesalers wouldn't take them. And then Dave Bradshaw had no money to buy goods to fill his store. All he had was Prosperity Bonds and the wholesalers wouldn't take them.

This Aberhart was a preacher in Calgary. He was full of wind, you know. He was gonna print paper just like they did in Germany to increase purchasing power. But purchasing power has to represent goods and service. And he had nothing behind it. This was in 1936. Depth of the Depression. It was a *crazy* idea. Folded up in about six months, this Funny Money business.

Jack Hallett,
Federal, Alberta

THEY WERE KICKED OFF AND THEY WERE HUNGRY

We're on the main line from Winnipeg to Saskatoon, and we'd get a lot of these hobos. This was an inspection point when the freight came out of Dauphin. Inspection means that the brakemen would run along each side of the train and check every wheel bearing, put a shot of oil in each bearing. If a bearing was hot, they'd shunt the car off to prevent the axle from breaking, which would derail the car. The train would spend maybe 15 minutes here for inspection. So they'd get off and come running over to the store, want a loaf of bread or a slice of bread. And Dad was the kind that would never refuse anybody.

A lot of times they had no money at all. Dad would give them a slice of bread and a slab of bologna and that would be their supper. We'd have 10 or 15 a day at the height of the Depression. But the Good Lord was good to us. What you give away like that you never miss. You get it back.

They would never do any vandalism. They were always polite. I remembr a few times, the conductors on the freight trains would get mean, go along and kick everybody off. We'd have four or five guys, kicked off, sitting here waiting for the next train, hoping the next conductor would not be so mean. They'd come over and tell us they were kicked off and they were hungry.

Bill Mason,
Makinak, Manitoba

AND WAVED GOODBYE

In 1933 when the store was bought, there were cars, but a lot of cars were turned into "Bennett Buggies". They were no longer serviceable, or cost money to repair. What people did was junk the engines, take off the front, make it as light as

Bennett buggies (cars converted into horse-drawn carriages and named after Prime Minister Bennett) were symptomatic of the Depression on the Prairies, when no one could afford gasoline. They were also symbolic of man's ingenuity and sense of fun in the worst of times. This one is in Biggar, Saskatchewan.

possible, put a tongue on it and have a team of horses pulling it. And there you went.

There was nobody starving in this area, but there were children that had hardly any clothes to go to school. And some had a very poor diet. There were beef rings that went around. You would donate an animal this week and it was cut up, and different people used it. And somebody else would donate one next week. So you always had fresh meat. The fellow who butchered got some meat for his services . . . and it gave him a job.

At that time there were people actually leaving the land, just walking right out of the house. Two miles down the road, the people . . . I don't know how they got the money, but they bought a car; the land they didn't sell, nobody would buy it and they probably didn't own it because there were back taxes. Got in the car and waved goodbye when they went past the school, and I've never seen them since. That was 1936, Headed for British Columbia.

Bob Hallett,
Federal, Alberta

CHAPTER EIGHT

MARK IT ON THE BOOK

Credit was a way of life at the country store. A farmer's finances followed the flow of the seasons. In the spring, his pockets were sparse and bare like his fields. In the fall, if his harvest was good, his pockets were full and he paid his debt at the village store.

Marking it on the book was time-consuming, confusing and often subject to dispute. Many a storekeeper, after a long day of physical work, had to face the books late at night. Sometimes his or her head didn't work so well while trying to add up and make sense of someone's complicated account. How much wood did we take on Abe's account? How much did we allow him for the turkeys we took in trade? How long since he paid any cash? Were we letting his bill get too high? Was this a good time to ask him for money?

A whole range of expressions covered the rural preoccupation with credit. Goods would be given "on credit, marked on the book, put on the tick, on account, on the tab". A customer might say, "See you next fall," or "See you Sunday." The storekeeper would be "carrying the customer". Either the wholesaler or the storekeeper might be "tightening up, clamping down, putting the squeeze on".

In the fall, the customer would come in to "settle up, wipe out the debt, get out of the red", or "in the clear", to "pay you off, get it off the books", or "straighten up".

One merchant would call another to check on a new customer who wanted credit. He might find out that the customer in question was "poor as Jobe's Turkey, no good, crooked" or "a bad risk". A good customer was "solid, a good bet, all right".

It was part and parcel of storekeeping to know whom you could trust and whom you couldn't. If you misjudged too often, you went under. Newcomers to an area were particularly risky. When a new company or a naval base brought in new faces, you had no yardstick to measure them by. "If you were smart enough, you'd cut them off after they'd stick you for one month. But sometimes you'd carry them on for another month and there'd be a double stick."

Many accounts were "written off" as you faced the fact that So-and-So never intended to pay or had left the country. Sometimes you could "garnishee" his wages if you could find the man and if he had a job. Sometimes you would turn the account over to a collection agency, but often the agency knew less about Joe Blow than you did and would be less likely to get any money. Or you could wait 20 years until times were better, and hope they'd pay.

Some did. There are stories of storekeepers hopping from foot to foot, humming and hawing because they knew they had thrown out the bill and here was the man wanting to pay it. Usually they would say they'd misplaced it for the moment, and the customer would say he knew the exact amount and here it was, and all ended happily.

Strangers who wanted gas were a particular problem. If you didn't demand payment first, they would drive off into the sunset and leave you holding the empty pump. In some cases, strangers with no money would leave a watch or a ring and come back for it later. One man left Katie McLeod a spare tire. "We had it there for a long time until the dealer he bought it from called us. It seemed the dealer had never been paid for it and he wanted it back."

In spite of artful schemes thought up by a few merchants like Albert Emond in Ontario and John Green in Alberta, most storekeepers, when asked if they had any good ways of collecting bills, replied emphatically, "Not in my time!"

PLEASE KEEP THIS BILL FOR REFERENCE

Bought of

M. R. SWERDFEGER
Dry Goods, Groceries, Boots and Shoes
Flour, Feed, Hardware, Gas and Oil

Glen Stewart, _Sept 18_ 1929

M.r. _Jas Gilmer_

	PHONE 110 R 5	Account Forwarded		
1	1 pr overalls		1	00
2	1 denim smock	2	25	
3	8 gal gas 22¢	1	76	
4	5 lbs sugar		30	
5	1 corn starch		16	
6	1 kim strap		28	
7	6 4" bolts		12	
8	4 loaves bread (round)		25	
9	1 gal coal oil		12	
10	1 set single harness	29	00	
11	4 rolls wall paper	1	20	
12	6 yards prints 23¢	1	38	
13		37	82	
14	Credit 30 doz eggs 12¢	3	60	
15	23 Chg.	34	22	

THE IROQUOIS POST, IROQUOIS, ONT. X

I HAD TO PAY FOR HIS DENTURES

*I*f anyone was short of cash, they came and asked for some just as if it was a glass of water. A customer came in and said. "Give me $100, I'm going to a sale to buy cows!" Another one asked for $50 because his father-in-law had died in New Brunswick. A dentist refused credit to a man, and I had to pay for his dentures. But with all these different incidents, I never lost a dollar. I found I could trust nearly everyone in the community.

*Milton Swerdfeger,
Glen Stewart, Ontario*

'TIL THE FIRST OF NOVEMBER

*M*cNaughton's gave credit. Unbelievable today. Right from the time he started, you didn't pay McNaughton 'til the first of November. You'd get your crop off and some of it sold before they'd ask you to pay.

They certainly made a tremendous contribution to this country by giving credit. They did their part in the '30s when people were desperate. The drought. It was bad here. But a lot worse other places. The main line was sort of the dividing line. North of the railway, not too bad. South, real bad. McNaughton's had a heart, no doubt about that. They themselves toted a tremendous line of credit at the bank. It's hard to believe that they would have an overdraft of a quarter million dollars, without even a note signed.

Oh, they had to have some losses. Some homesteaders just simply vanished. But obviously it couldn't have been too serious because they continued to flourish. It was amazing how much commerce was done with so little money.

*Bert McKay,
Moosomin, Saskatchewan*

THE HONESTY OF PEOPLE

*T*he honesty of most people is amazing. One man mailed me 50¢ for fruit he had stolen one day when he was hungry and desperate.

One day last year when I was playing cribbage at the Legion, a man tapped me on the shoulder, "You're Joe Cony, aren't you?"

"Yes."

"Well, I owe you money and here's $50. I know that my bill was under $50."

I didn't recognize him. I still have no idea who he is. But it bothered him that he owed me and he was paying up . . . maybe from 20 years ago.

Joe Cony,
Rocky Mountain House, Alberta

MAN'S FAITH IN MAN

*T*he outport businessman was everything to everybody, because there was no cheque from the government.

A small minority would have starved. That small minority was saved by the merchants. If you have a man coming to your store at 10 o'clock saying he, his wife and family have had no breakfast, what are you going to do? All his dried fish has been sold already to pay his account.

There was no competition among the merchants. We each had our own customers. But there was one merchant here who bartered fish, but didn't supply any credit. If one of your fishermen had some fish ready to ship, you knew how much fish he had because you knew how much salt he had . . . but someone would come to the store and say, "I saw So-and-So shipping to Emmanuel."

When he came back to us, we'd say, "I understand you shipped fish to Emmanuel that you were supposed to ship to us."

"Well sir, me wife wanted a pair of shoes, and you wouldn't let her have it."

When they'd come and want something like a new dress, we'd say, "Now let's wait a little while because you're not getting much fish." These were the people we had to keep from starving during the winter.

If there was a bad fishery, you were in the same category as the fisherman. If he didn't get the fish to pay you, you didn't have the fish to export and you couldn't pay your supplier. My brother, Harry, one time went to St. John's and we had two schooner loads of fish, the *Lone Flyer* and the *Edna Louise*, and he could not get 5¢ for that fish. They would only take it on condition that he turn it in on account. They would take so much against the debt and give him some foodstuffs. It took us years to catch up on those debts, but eventually we paid them all off.

The outport merchant was the fisherman's lawyer, his advisor, his friend. If he had a good reputation with the suppliers in St. John's, he was in a position to help them because he could get his help, too.

Dun and Bradstreet at one time had a little logo on their stationery: "CREDIT: MAN'S FAITH IN MAN".

Bill Ashbourne and Herb Gillett,
Twillingate, Newfoundland

EATON'S CATALOGUE

Oh, we can't forget Eaton's! Eaton's had the variety which we couldn't carry. When we were pricing goods, we often used to check Eaton's price. They were the big competitor. But you paid cash.

I remember a story about Eaton's: a farmer came in for a hammer and the storekeeper said "$1.95". This farmer says, "Well, I can buy it from Eaton's for almost a dollar less."

So the storekeeper says, "That's fine. I'll sell it to you for that and you come back in a week and get it." You see you had to order it, and buy the money order and then wait for it from Eaton's.

S.A. Sigurdson,
Arborg, Manitoba

GIVE ME $10

This fellow owed him money and he was no good, he never intended to pay. It made Albert mad that he had put one over on him. It was about $10 that he owed and Albert made out a bill for $45 and sent it to him.

So the fellow comes in roaring mad, "I don't owe you any $45, all I owe you is $10!"

Albert said, "Well then, give me $10."

"If I do, will you mark this paid?"
Albert said, "Sure."
So he paid the $10.

Doris Emond,
Camborne, Ontario

THE WHOLESALERS

*T*he wholesalers were very good, they didn't clamp down on you, they'd give you time to clean up your accounts. Groceries were our biggest item. And possibly, in the early days, flour and feed. And we also handled coal. And wood. We'd get carloads in, in the fall of the year; we'd solicit the district for orders first, then we'd get a carload.

When the wholesalers started tightening up, we had to tighten up. I had one fellow who left here owing me around $300. Said he didn't have any money to pay me, but he would send me money every month. And there wasn't a month that he missed sending me $10 until the account was cleaned up.

Arthur Burch,
Wynndel, British Columbia

DRAW IT IN THE BOOK

A guy by the name of Louis was clerking down at Peter Smythe's store. He didn't have much education, couldn't read or write, but he could figure things out pretty well in his head. In those days it was mostly barter anyway.

Somebody bought a grinding stone from him. So Louis drew a picture in the book to charge it to the man's name. Then this man came in to pay his bill about a month later and wanted to know why it was so high. Louis said, "Well, you bought a cake of cheese here."

"No. I never bought any cheese."

So they went over the things he had bought and it finally came out that he had bought a grindstone.

Louis said, "Oh my gosh, I forgot to put the hole in the middle!"

Joe MacIsaac,
Port Hood, Nova Scotia

Sullivan's store in the Irish Catholic community of Ennismore, Ontario was a place where you came after Sunday Mass to do your weekly shopping. If you had bought "this and that" through the week, you would "settle up" on Sunday.

SEE YOU SUNDAY

*E*nnismore is an Irish Roman-Catholic settlement near Peterborough, Ontario. Fifty years ago, our entire community went to Mass on a Sunday morning, then directly to Crough's or Sullivan's general stores. Actually, the women reached the store first, while the men lingered around the church sheds for a smoke. Men straggled in later to pay the bills for goods their wives had bought.

"See you Sunday," was, in those days, as good as a promissory note. It meant that goods picked up through the week would be paid for on Sunday when the main shopping would be done.

Jean Cavanagh,
Ennismore, Ontario

PRICE IT TO PAW

*A*t one time when we wanted to get something at the store on credit, we would say, "Price it to Paw." That was because of Ernie Boulder and his brothers. Their father was said to be very, very close. They lived in the Hollow there and they wouldn't have the money, so they'd come to Andy in the store and say, "Oh, price it to Paw." That would mean, "Charge it to Father."

And Paw would have no intention of paying because he was real close. It would be real hard to get old Paw Boulder to pay for it.

New Brunswick

FORGIVE AND FORGET

*T*he government came to the aid of the farmers in the Depression. There was a Farmers Creditors Arrangement Act. Say somebody owed us $100. (In those days a farmer could be sold out for about $100, because nobody wanted to buy a farm anyway.) So the government would come to us and say, "How much does this farmer owe you?"

"$100."

"Well, he will pay you in so many payments in three or four years, but you will have to forgive him half of that bill."

There were some farmers that, when times were good again, would come and say, "Now we're going to pay that half of the bill we still owe you."

But there were others who forgot all about it.

Katie MacLeod,
Vernon River, Prince Edward Island

DAMNED LUCKY

*I*t wasn't easy. People didn't have money and my father carried a lot of them on credit. Some of them, he never did get the money. And they'd get quite lippy too. I can remember one kid . . . the whole family were hard up, a pretty tough bunch. This kid was quite brazen. She came in and asked for an order of stuff. Dad did it up for her and he said, "When are you gonna pay for it?"

She grabbed it and she says, "You'll be damned lucky if you ever get paid!"

Jean (Weir) Drimmie,
Lang, Ontario

On raised wooden counter boxes, such as this one in Alvena, Saskatchewan, storekeepers put it "on the bill" or "on the book" and waited until the harvest was reaped before being paid.

WHAT YOU GIVE AWAY

Oh yes, he gave credit. I often think how he used to deal with people. If they wanted a pound of something, it would probably end up to be a pound and a quarter. If they wanted a dozen staples to fix their fence, he would get a handful of staples and give it to them for the same price. Yet business seemed to flourish.

The people knew he had nothing when he started. But they knew he had to have some money to order more things . . . and they would *try*. Or if they had no money, they would bring him something else, from the garden, or something he could use, like wood.

What he gave away to people didn't seem to hurt him at all, it seemed to help if anything.

Corine (McGarry) Stillborn,
Finnie, Saskatchewan

IN MY LITTLE OLD CAR

Gill carried a lot of people, believe me. No, he didn't have any good ways to collect! But after I married him, I decided to try.

I went to this nice, posh place down in the city, went right up to her door. She was so taken back, she didn't believe it. And she was so haughty.

I said, "I beg your pardon, but I was left a widow too and I had to pay my bills. So you can pay yours now."

So then she decided she'd better pay. She knew she owed it. Gill had been really good to them and helped them when they needed help.

I collected quite a few that summer . . . took my little old car and went around and got a little bit at a time. My incentive was that Gill said, anything I could collect, I could have.

I might have done better to pick raspberries. But there was some satisfaction, too.

Melva Roberts,
Long Reach, New Brunswick

BURYING THE BILLS

J.B.M. St. Laurent, the father of Prime Minister Louis St. Laurent, kept store in Compton, Quebec. His son, Maurice, took over the store, then his son, Marc, who was my husband.

The Depression was hard on the St. Laurent store. Maurice was a very generous man; there were a lot of big families and he couldn't see anybody go hungry.

My assistant at the post office now says if it hadn't been for Maurice St. Laurent buying meal bags from her, she would not have her school diploma. You had to pay so much for writing your exams to get your diploma. He would give 5¢ or 10¢ a bag. She says she knows very well he didn't use them, just took them to help her.

There were a lot of bills that Maurice never collected . . . thousands of dollars. When Marc and I closed the store in 1969, because the government wanted it for an historic site, we buried the bills. I said to Marc, "Why not burn them?"

"No, we'll dig a hole."

At one time his father had mentioned some sort of law

against burning bills. So we put them in the ground. Buried them right beside the store.

Mary St. Laurent,
Compton, Quebec

BAD DEBTS IN THE WINDOW

*W*e wrote off an average of $1000 a year for 32 years in Pincher Creek. That was a lot when butter used to be 50¢ a pound. I collected bad debts once by putting them in the window. It antagonized an awful lot of people.

They were all sent a registered letter and there was an ad put in the paper saying that 30 days from now, these names would be publicized within the store. So I got a blackboard and wrote them all down. I didn't get any black eyes about it. But some people were very angry.

Those with any pride came in and paid to avoid having the family name blemished in public. But a lot of people couldn't care less. "Let him go ahead. He can't collect anyhow!"

I collected a few debts, but I didn't make any friends. It was a poor idea.

John Green,
Pincher Creek, Alberta

GETTING HIS FISH

*E*very merchant had a bunch of fishermen. The fishermen would build boats and get ready for the spring fishery. The merchant would supply them. If it was a good fishery, the merchant came out all right. If it was a bad fishery, he'd have to carry them over to the next year . . . they depended on the merchant for food.

Father never hauled a man to court for debt in his life. If he couldn't pay it, Father would write it off. But he did collect his fish. Some of the guys, when they'd see his boat coming out to collect, would lock up their storehouses and take to the woods. But Father would go to the storehouse, break the lock and weigh the fish . . . they were his fish because he had paid for them with supplies.

Gus Hayes,
Stephenville, Newfoundland

CHAPTER NINE

HUNGRY FOR THE NEWS

If you went to the store often enough, you could find out almost anything. News of the local community was shared by word of mouth or by auction sale bills and church social announcements tacked on the door. News of the greater world came by stage coach or dog-team or mail boat or rail to the post office tucked in a corner of the store, or to a telegraph station; or a "telephony box" on the wall.

By 1789, Upper Canada had eight post offices, all on the main post roads along the Front (the lands adjacent to the St. Lawrence and Lake Ontario). By 1867, post offices were spread across the country. Added to the warmth, hospitality and general excitement of the crossroads store was the possibility that there might be a letter there from some far distant place with your name on it.

Until recent years, the Canadian public looked upon its postal service with awe and admiration. Storekeepers tumbled out of bed at 7 a.m. and raced for the train with a heavy bag of mail; or they would wait up late at night and haul it home in a blinding blizzard. On coastal inlets and on half-frozen lakes, dog-team drivers risked their lives at freeze-up and break-up times to bring in the mail. Waiting for the mail in remote rural settlements was a Canadian pastime which had a social significance comparable to going to the theatre in larger city centres.

During the First World War, the telegraph operator, who was often located in the store, played a grim role in bringing in news of war casualties, as well as battles lost or won. ''She got it all by telegraph,'' Gus Hayes of Newfoundland remembers, ''and wrote it all down. Sometimes two pages and a half a day.''

In 1877, the Canadian patent was issued on ''Bell's System of Telephony''. Telephone poles carried lines from Montreal to Kingston by 1885. The first phones appeared in country stores. Later, the logical place to put a switchboard was in the local store. John Leacy's grocery store in Cardinal

This post office operating at Century Village, Lang, Ontario is typical of ones to be found in Canadian stores since the 1800s.

was truly a news-clearing house with post office, telegraph office and telephone exchange. P.G. Towns at Douro, Ontario had a telephone exchange, served as postmaster, township treasurer and local fire department. When news came in by telephone of a house or barn on fire, it was the Towns' truck which raced out with its varied collection of firefighters mustered by Central.

By the 1920s, many rural houses had their own phones. The Bell Telephone Company installed its 500 000th telephone in 1924. But in 1931, more phones were disconnected than installed, as the Depression made luxuries untenable.

Usually the crossroads store managed to keep its phone and keep the district in touch with the rest of the world. In some western communities like Halkirk and Fleet in Alberta, "barbed wire telephone systems" carried news out to rural households after it reached the store. "It worked. Not too good. But it worked."

Across Canada, switchboard operators or "Centrals" were usually women. Mrs. Lily Hudson at Boulter, Ontario operated the switchboard there for 41 years. When she retired in 1946 to a house across the road, she took the switchboard with her.

Operators like Lily Hudson held the whole community in their hands. Central and her party-line system could get help to a child with appendicitis or save a house from burning, a mother from having her baby alone, or a man from bleeding to death from an axe cut.

The party line also shattered the debilitating loneliness which plagued women and older folk on isolated back roads. "Listening-in" on the party line was taken for granted in early, less-sophisticated days. While busy people had little time for such nonsense, cripples and shut-ins and chronically lonely people did. The party line was a kind of pre-television soap opera for them, an added dimension to their too-quiet lives.

Mrs. Richard Dingman in her post office at Codrington store. Codrington was an important stop on the stage route from Brighton to Campbellford in southern Ontario.

THE LUCK OF THE IRISH

*W*e kept the Post Office as well as a General Store. The postage in those days was very high, ranging from four and half pence to three shillings in Canada, according to the distance; to the Old Country it was as high as six shillings and seven shillings. On one occasion a letter came from Ireland for one Wm. Armstrong, Trafalgar, the postage on which was seven shillings. One day when I had been left alone, I saw a rough looking Irishman coming down the concession on a white horse. He drew up at the door and asked, "Is there ever a letter for Wm. Armstrong?" I brought it out and handed it to him and told him the amount of the postage to be paid. He asked if I thought it was for him, and I said, "Certainly, if your name's Wm. Armstrong." He replied, "That's my name, open it." I told him he must open it. This he did and asked me to "rade" it. I read it over and where I could not make out the names, he would pronounce them for me, as many of them were new and outlandish to me. After I read it once, he said, "Rade it again." This I proceeded to do and when I had finished he said, "That

Loafers, as they were lovingly called, were people who stayed in the store, not to buy but to listen, to visit, to tell stories and jokes, to share whatever it meant to be part of this particular village in this part of Canada.

letter isn't for me at all. You must put it back in the office.'' And to my amazement he strolled off leaving the postage of seven shilling unpaid.

*from Peter Robinson Jarvis diary,
Hazel Matthews papers,
Oakville Historical Society,
Oakville Museum,
Oakville, Ontario*

SECOND-HAND NEWS

*I*n my day, the store was the place to go in the evening. They would go out into the field opposite and pitch horseshoes and

then they'd gather in the store. There were nail kegs that they sat on and benches and old boxes turned over, and they'd all have a big story to tell. Outside, there were benches out of the old schoolhouse. In summer, they sat there and the horses were tethered down at the end where there was a barn.

They'd keep the store open until 11:30 or so, talking every night. That's where everybody found out about everybody else along The Reach, and they couldn't live if they didn't get to the store.

It was the men that would go to the store at night. The women only got what news they were told.

Zaidee William,
Long Reach, New Brunswick

They sat on stools, cracker barrels, kitchen chairs, benches or counters; they leaned on overalls or blankets or candy showcases, on soft-drink coolers in later years. They ate bologna and crackers and cheese and chocolate bars, drank apple cider, Coke, Pepsi, Orange Crush and Canada Dry. This is Bentley's store in Lethbridge, Alberta in 1899.

SOMETHING WE WILL NEVER SEE AGAIN

*T*he postal service in Fleet was something we will never see again. Max Slemp, he was the postmaster and the store operator. The train went through here six days a week. It left Coronation, where it stayed overnight, heading west for Lacombe. Max was up at 6:20 a.m. when the train went through, for as long as the train was running a mail service . . . over 25 years. He carried the mail on his back down to the station.

At 5:20 in the afternoon the train came in again. The train sat there to connect with the Edmonton-Calgary run. You could go up there at 6 o'clock or anytime after, up to 10 or 11 at night, and you could get your mail. That meant you had mail service from 7 in the morning 'til 10 at night, six days a week.

A letter mailed in Calgary in the morning got here . . . 200 miles by rail . . . in the late afternoon. I mailed a letter here one day and got a reply back from Calgary the same day. Now I live within 30 miles of Calgary and get postal service five times a week, and if I mail a letter to Calgary, the service to Calgary and back is approximately one week. We used to get a daily paper, the Calgary *Herald*, here, the day it was printed. Two years ago I quit the daily paper where I live because we got Saturday's paper on Tuesday.

Bob Hallett,
Coronation, Alberta

THE BACKBONE OF THE COMMUNITY

*T*hey depended on me very much in the post office we had in the Valley River store, especially when the older people were around. I was their interpreter, I was their letter writer, I was their advisor, I was their . . . sort of right-hand man.

Because a lot of them could not speak the English language, there was a language barrier. And, of course, a lot of parcels went out to Europe at that time, back to Russia. And I used to write their letters; I'm quite fluent in Ukrainian and I can read and write it. I wrote their letters. I addressed their letters. I fixed their parcels up, and they always got there. I had the reputation of being able to send parcels.

They could write Ukrainian, but I think they felt it wasn't

legible enough. And being postmistress in a small community like that, you're sort of like the old-time school teacher, the backbone of the community.

Olga Petreshan,
Valley River, Manitoba

A RISKY JOB

*O*ur newspapers on the west coast of Newfoundland were the *Western Star* and the *Daily News* and the *Family Herald*. People would read every word of the *Family Herald*. A good family paper. Always had a serial in it. Everybody felt so bad when the *Family Herald* went out.

Our mail came in summertime by mail boat, in wintertime by dog team from Deer Lake. That was the nearest railway station to this coast. Thomas Knott was the man who drove the mail on this coast from the time I was a young boy until he got too old. Then his son, Jim, took over.

It would take about three days to get here . . . get to Bonne Bay the first day, next day to Woody Point, then across the bay, then the next day it would get here. Sometimes Bonne Bay wasn't frozen well, and they had an awful job to get the mail across.

But they got it across every week. A risky job. More than once they fell through the ice. There would always be two of them on the mail team. If one fellow fell in, the other would pull him out.

Gordon Spears,
Rocky Harbour, Newfoundland

THE MAIL POLE

*T*o get the mail for Magwire, we would wait at the nearest crossing for the train to come. There was a pole with an arm stretching out over the track and on this we would hang the bag of mail. The train would slow down, but never stop. A man on the train would grab the bag of mail as the train went by, and throw off the new bag for us.

Cy Strange,
Magwire, Ontario

YOU'D SWEAR I WAS A CAMEL

*I*n our village it was a ritual that everybody came into town on
train day. Train day was three days a week. They'd come in
long before the train would arrive and do their business, and
just wait for the mail to be sorted. We'd have 25 people sitting
around while we're sorting the mail. The whole town would be
quite busy. The rest of the time you could shoot a cannon down
the main street and not hit a cat. But I could have used five
clerks some days right through the mail period up to seven or
eight o'clock at night.

When the train came back from Rocky Mountain House,
about 7:15 in the morning, I had to take our outgoing mail and
put it on the train. Loose mail would be placed in the slot in the
store door during the night, and I would take that in my hand
along with the mail bags and parcels. I'd be stacked up with
five or six bags on my back going down to the station, a
hundred yards away.

I remember one harrowing experience when we heard the
train coming about a quarter mile from the village. We had
overslept. So I pull on a pair of pants and, racing down the
stairs, I pick up loose mail in one hand, heave the five bags of
mail onto my shoulder with the other hand. By the time I start
down to the station, the train has arrived and is taking off
again. So I run very hard kitty-corner across the common to
catch it. And I throw everything (bags and some of the letters)
on the steps of the caboose for the trainman. Then I pick up
loose letters all the way back up the hill, because I couldn't
keep them in my hand.

Carrying the mail was a real agony for years. At Christmas
time you'd swear I was a camel. I'd make three or four trips,
just loaded with these big bags for both the incoming and
outgoing mail. For about two weeks we would have enormous
mail comparable to a town 10 times the size of our village.

Don Wilkes,
Benalto, Alberta

TELEGRAPHIC CHECKERS

I was to a meeting at the little church. Mr. W.D. Stalker was to
the meeting. His father and uncle lived in Port Ryerse and said

that a hundred years ago they would meet at the store at night and play checkers. They had a telegraphic system between Port Ryerse and Vittoria and that was how they would play back and forth. I thought from the way he spoke they must have had a great time, a better time than at the store now.

Omar Thompson,
Port Ryerse, Ontario

THE RADIOTELEPHONE SYSTEM

*T*he first radio was sold in the area by the Knutsford store to George Abear, and was listened to by the use of earphones. Soon after George got it, he thought of a plan for all those who had a telephone to hear the radio.

On the party-line system, long and short rings were cranked out to call the desired person. At that time three long rings was not assigned to anybody. So by prearranging a time, and cranking out three long rings, he held the earphone close to the telephone microphone, and everybody picked up their receivers and listened to the radio. Probably for the first time.

Stanley Finbow,
Knutsford, British Columbia

BARBED-WIRE TELEPHONE LINE

*O*ne particular store in Fleet . . . Max Slemp's . . . had the regular Alberta Government telephone system. The barbed-wire system tried to tie on to the government line, but it was not up to standard. So they negotiated with Max Slemp and they put the "mother phone" on one of his walls there.

So he'd have two phones; one phone would ring, or the other, and he knew which phone to answer by the sound of the chime. He'd relay messages through the existing government line to the barbed-wire line. Sometimes both receivers would be down and he'd be hopping from one to the other relaying the message.

It was a very satisfactory system if somebody didn't pull the wire down or somebody's animals didn't go through it and cut the line. It was only three or four feet off the ground. Sometimes the wire connections were not that good. For insulators, they used a piece of rubber under every staple. But the barbed-wire telephone worked, and served the purpose from about 1935 until after the war was over. A 10-year period that it served.

Bob Hallett,
Coronation, Alberta

ELECTING LOUIS ST. LAURENT

People would sit around the old stove. A lot of funny things were told there, especially during a municipal or federal or

Outside the Stuckley store at Boulter, Ontario three local people pass the time of day.

provincial election. I remember when Uncle Louis ran for Prime Minister . . . all the journalists and photographers here taking pictures. We all felt sure he was going to win.

We got the news on the radio, and as polls closed all around, they would phone us. People came here and we had a big party in the town hall. Everybody came to the party whether they voted for or against him. But there were very few Conservative votes that first time.

My mother's parents were Conservative. They were farmers, and at one time they came to live with us. My father's sister said, "They'll get along all right, but if an election comes up, there will be some hot talking."

But when it came election time, by then my grandfather had become a Liberal. Because of Louis St. Laurent.

Mary St. Laurent
Compton, Quebec

SHE TOOK OFF HER APRON

*I*t took the old folks some time to get used to the phones. Maggie, my mother, used to say, "Now where is your phone in the house. If I can picture where you are standing, I can talk to you better."

There was one old lady here so shy of the phone, she would fix herself all up before she'd answer it. The young lads in the store rang up her number and went over to see what she'd do.

Before she picked it up, she combed her hair and took off her apron.

Walter Cameron,
Fallbrook, Ontario

CHAPTER TEN

THE STOVE IN THE STORE

The men would stamp snow off their boots in the veranda stoop before they opened the store door. Then they would head for the pot-bellied stove, shake their coonskin coats and make the hot stove sizzle with wet snow. Sometimes they wanted groceries or tobacco, sometimes they only wanted to "set a while".

Our stove was big and round with a silver bumper running around it. It was a living thing with a reckless personality that frequently got the pipes on fire, so it demanded constant attention and watchfulness, but was not loved any less for its antics. It was the centre of the store and it symbolized warmth and hospitality.

Charlie Anderson walked a mile to the store every night and tipped his chair back against the dry-goods counter . . . a quiet man who listened more than he talked. The night he went home, sat down, took off one boot, then fell off the chair and died, it was my Dad they phoned. Across Canada there were Charlie Andersons and Jonas Christophersons and Billy Smiths and Alec Kalinchuks and Nelse Tousants in every country store, respected older men whose knowledge of living enriched the conversation, or whose quiet chuckle pleased the younger story tellers.

Not all the stories told around the stove were true. My uncle used to say, "Are you listening? Well, if you're listening, then I'll tell you a good one!"

In order not to miss any good ones, I did my homework in the store. Our dry-goods counter jutted out just where the overalls were stacked, and formed a little ledge. There I stacked my homework books and then tipped my chair back between stove and counter with my feet on the silver bumper. It was a bit like kids doing homework today with the television on, but I got by. Possibly I learned more from the stories in the store than from the books.

When I went back to the Glen Stewart store with my father in 1980, the present storekeeper was saying how she had to install a little coffee table in the corner of her modernized store: "The older men seemed to want some place to sit and talk."

Dad and I didn't say anything. We were busy figuring where the stove used to sit, and finding the stove-pipe hole in the ceiling.

The Glen Stewart store as it looked in wintertime in the '30s, '40s and '50s. The wooden stoop appeared like magic in November and disappeared again in March. It protected the store from cold north-west winds. Inside, an enormous pot-bellied stove warmed the customers who gathered around it.

WARMTH IN THE WINTER NIGHT

Men who worked the snowploughs during the '30s and '40s stopped at the store for warmth any hour of the night. One driver, who got his plough through blocked roads to Glen Stewart in the middle of the night, was almost frozen. The heater in his truck had stopped working, and he said he wouldn't have stood the cold much longer.

Sometimes, the large county plough from Finch was called in to open Glen Stewart roads. Two men on that plough stopped in at two o'clock one night. Print was scarce at the time and the driver bought 43 yards. Then he spied a pig I had butchered and brought in frozen the evening before. He bought that, and I stood it up hump-backed in an empty Corn Flakes carton with its mouth open. He took it home frozen on the truck. Later, I heard that he set it in front of the stair steps to scare his wife when she came downstairs in the morning.

Milton Swerdfeger,
Glen Stewart, Ontario

COMING FOR TOBACCO

In winter, the roads would be closed and we'd have drifts 10 feet high. We would haul goods in by horse and sleigh. But there would rarely be a day when we wouldn't see somebody come to the store, even during the storms. I've had customers come in a real blizzard, make their way across a field on foot, for tobacco or sugar or tea.

You'd be looking out a window and wonder at this dark spot. Then, when the drifting eased, that would be a human being coming.

"Out of tobacco!"

Ben Cousins,
Rose Valley, Prince Edward Island

SOME PLACE TO KEEP WARM AND TO WAIT

Blizzards used to come every winter then. Sometimes people would have to wait until the snowplough would come through

before the train could get through. They had something that was like a snowmobile at Lemburg to get people back and forth to the trains in the wintertime — on skis, and it had its own engine. I can remember it bringing passengers to the train.

It didn't matter that much if the roads were blown in because people had horses anyway, but people did depend on the trains. The ones that got in trouble would be something to do with the trains. The trains would stop and they had to get some place to keep warm and to wait. Until they could plough out the tracks.

I can remember people staying in the store overnight. People could stay in the station, but sometimes Mother would feel sorry for them and say, "Well, they haven't had anything to eat." So she'd send someone over to tell them to come over and have something to eat. When they were there, the store was warm as well and they would probably stay until the train would come. She fed everyone who was in need.

Corine (McGarry) Stillborn,
Finnie, Saskatchewan

TWO HUNDRED FROM THE HIGHWAY

*W*e're on the 115, one of Ontario's busiest highways, and one that's famous for bad winter storms. So we've had people sleep in the store quite a few times. But the biggest time was in 1958.

It was a nice Sunday afternoon, people out with their kids and old folks for a Sunday drive. Then about three o'clock a blizzard came on and we ended up with 200 people here overnight.

We put the older people and the babies upstairs in the three bedrooms. The younger ones stayed awake or slept sitting up against a wall. We had a wood stove going in the kitchen and an oil stove in the store, and people everywhere. The living room was full, just a path open to the kitchen.

Some had a touch of the frostbite. One lady who'd had nursing experience was helping them out. We had five or six policemen here and they'd keep going out and bringing more people in. The women got busy and made sandwiches for everybody with cans of salmon and sliced meats.

Everyone was in great spirits. Even the dogs, which we put

◁ *Here, in Compton, Quebec, in the store of Maurice St. Laurent, is the typical loafing and laughter that was carried on wherever there was a hot stove in a country store.*

135

in the back room, got along pretty well, although one got snarly and I had to put the boots to him. Altogether, it was a night to remember.

Bill and Bob Reid,
Kirby, Ontario

SPRINGTIME IN ALBERTA

*W*hen winter comes here in Alberta, they toss the extra blankets and parkas in the trunk of the car and they stay there all winter. But they thought spring had come for sure, so they had cleared out their blankets. We were having the curling banquet at the end of the season, late spring.

We had left the kids at home to take the mail to the 8:30 train. Men came into the store and said, "I hear on the radio we're in for a storm!" Storms here come in quite quickly, and this one was a real bad blizzard.

After the banquet, some tried to get out to their places and had to turn back. So it ended up we had the store full of people and we fixed up beds upstairs for half a dozen extra, and the men just sat around the old pot-bellied stove all night.

Una Burley,
Brant, Alberta

THE STOVE-PIPE HOLE

*M*y sister and I slept directly over the store. It was the warmest bedroom in the house because the stove-pipe came up from the stove below. On a January night, you could warm your pillow on that pipe before you crawled in.

A round grate encircled the stove-pipe. For fun, you could drop bits of paper down through that grate onto the customers below. Bald-headed ones were the most fun.

Sundays were rather boring days for my sister and I because the people were all gone. Also, on Sundays there would be no fire in the stove in the store. I can remember how cold it would be going up the stairs to our bedrooms over the store. It always seemed so nice to get back to Monday morning.

Enid Swerdfeger,
Glen Stewart, Ontario

WITH A BIT OF A SCOLD

*T*he main fun for a boy was the fact that every night the local men would congregate for chats, smokes, yarns and some small purchases. The store was a big white-brick, square-fronted, two-storey house with a warehouse on one side, a living projection on the other and large kitchen built on the back. We lived mostly in the kitchen, but when I went to bed in the part over the store, I could lie over the grate that brought heat from the old-fashioned stove in the store . . . and listen to the talk. Many times my mother would come up and find me asleep and simply put me to bed with a bit of a scold.

Harry J. Boyle,
St. Augustine, Ontario

Stoves and counters were often quite beautiful in country stores. The combination of warmth, carved and polished wood, and objects which you wanted to buy, could make a store a place of rapturous delight. This is a Hudson's Bay Company store in Fort Vermilion, Alberta.

BEAR STORY

Around here there's a lot of Smiths and most of them are noted for being story tellers. One day, I had most of them in the store at once and they got trying to top one another. At the last of it, they were out in the dooryard and no one wanted to leave for fear he'd be topped. Charlie was there, and Tommy Alfred and others . . . I remember Charlie's bear story.

Charlie always had a moose or a deer or a bear tied up in his yard. He lived down in the hollow and was a great one to trap and hunt and he always had unusual things happen to him. So he came home this night . . . he was a section man on the railway . . . and his wife, Lena, said, "Your young bear is gone."

"I can't believe that. I had him well tied!" So anyway, he thought he'd go out along Birchard's Road and see if he could find him.

So Charlie went out and there he was up a tree. So he said, he tried and tried and tried, called him by name and he wouldn't come down. So he said, "Well, I'll go up and get him!" So he went up the tree. And he said the bear scratched and clawed at him something awful all the way down.

And he said, when he finally got it home, his own bear was there.

J.W. McNeil and Aubrey Bird,
Arthurette, New Brunswick

ALL LIARS HERE

There was a little store at Milville and the men were all sitting around there telling stories, when a stranger came in. And he wanted to know if there was any good hunting around there.

"Oh yes," they told him, "lots of good hunting . . . deer and moose. We never have any shortage of wild meat."

Then the fellow said, "Do you know who you are talking to? You are talking to the game warden."

The local man came right back with, "Well, do you know who you're talking to? You're talking to the biggest liar in the country."

Harry Hatfield,
Simonds, New Brunswick

CHARLIE'S MOOSE STORY

Charlie Smith had a moose story he told in the store, and I know that story was true. Charlie was out fishing for salmon in a brook, and this moose came out of the woods and stepped into the brook right beside him. He wondered at first if it was going to attack him. But then he walked up to the moose and started petting it.

He came into the store later and said, "Would you believe that I led a moose home?" Charlie said he led it by the ear, but he told somebody else that he went up to the barn and got a halter. Anyway, he had a little barn or driving shed, and you could go and see his moose in there.

The moose was stone blind. They get these ticks which can get into their blood stream and make them blind. Charlie kept it for a while, then the Lands and Forests people came and took it.

Aubrey Bird,
Arthurette, New Brunswick

DON'T BOTHER TO TELL ME

The women didn't used to go to the store that much. Grandpa, when he was not on the boats, went every night to the store in Harwood. So the men did the shopping. Mother, I don't think she was in that store half a dozen times. Grandpa would go there and sit and visit, and then he would come home with the stories . . . and sometimes they were stories Mother didn't want to hear.

Sarah Davy,
Harwood, Ontario

KNOCK-OUT

It was the boxing match where Joe Louis knocked Billy Conn cold in the first minute. Grant's Corners was ready for that 1946 match. All the men and quite a few of us kids were gathered at Annis McDonald's general store. The radio was on and the Coke cooler had been filled with beer. The men were

This slender pot-bellied stove warmed a store in Mille Roches, Ontario.

ready for a great night. We kids had been given Cokes and told to play outside on the store veranda.

Well, it was all over in the first minute. The fathers came out and took us home and they were really cross, their evening ruined. When we got home, all the mothers had gathered together to quilt, and they weren't pleased either. They said, "What are you fellows doing home so soon?" Their peaceful evening of quilting had been ruined too.

Alan Sheets
Grant's Corners, Ontario

THE KIRBY SENATE

*T*he Kirby Senate started meeting in our old store across the highway eight or nine years ago: a group of farmers and some businessmen who like to get together and chew the fat and laugh a little and discuss where Ottawa is going wrong. We even have one Ottawa senator coming in sometimes. When the group gets really hot about something the politicians are doing or not doing, off goes a petition to Ottawa.

Two years ago the Kirby Senate survived a move across Highway 115 to our new larger store. They not only survived, they celebrated, presenting us with a beautiful eight-foot pine table for the store. So that's what they sit around for their morning session now.

On a good morning, we'll go through 40 cups of coffee.

Bill and Bob Reid,
Kirby, Ontario

TRIBUTE

I was very much grieved on seeing the death notice of Mrs. Brooks. She was our very best friend in our childhood days. I am a veteran of the First World War. My only pleasant recollection of my childhood days is of those spent in her store, being one of a family of six whose parents were honest but of small means.

We were taken every Saturday to Mrs. Brooks' store where we were left in her care, while my father and mother did their shopping.

In the winter, if we were cold, we were put on chairs or sat on the floor around a big wood stove to keep warm. If our feet were cold, our shoes were taken off and feet .armed. If stockings needed repa around a big wood stove to keep warm. If our feet were cold, our shoes were taken off and feet warmed. If stockings needed repairs we were given new hand-knit stockings, also mitts. New clothes were made to fit us from clothes she collected from her neighbours.

We did not have clothes to go to church as other children, so Mrs. Brooks taught us not to feel badly if we could not go to church. God was every place we were and He loved us just the same.

She was the only Santa Claus we ever knew. She sent candies, cakes, fruit and something each one of us could wear.

These were the only gifts we ever received until we were old enought to go to work. When I went overseas I received her box every month as long as I was there and that was two years.

I am not speaking for myself alone but for the rest of the family scattered all over the province. I know they will feel the same when they learn of the loss of our loved friend.

We are not the only family. She was good to everyone. People like her are seldom born and as I lie on my hospital bed where I have been for 10 years, I am deeply grieved.

I feel that she is very near to me today and her thoughts will, I hope, help me to be worthy of such a friend.

B.J.W.
Toronto, Ontario (from Bobcaygeon
History *by Dorothe Comber)*

LIKE LAUREL AND HARDY

*W*e had a pot-bellied stove and we'd have chimney fires. I remember Father getting up on the roof to put them out. Once, I nearly killed myself laughing because he slipped and came scooting down the roof on his rear end and scooting off the roof. And he landed in a snowbank like Laurel and Hardy.

Cy Strange,
Magwire, ontario

STOVE-PIPE DAY

*O*h, I'll never forget taking the pipes down to clean. That was the biggest fight. We would fight like cats and dogs on stove-pipe day. Putting them back up was cleaner, but they'd never go together right . . . bang them and hammer them and curse at them, then tie them up with a piece of wire. When we got done, I always thought, "Thank God, we don't have to do that for another six months!"

I remember only one time when my husband really laughed while he was doing it. Our pipes came out of the stove and over to the stairwell. They came out in an L over the stairwell and then across upstairs into the chimney, and they were tied with a wire for support over the stairwell. Someow Bill untied this wire and it was so heavy with soot that it fell right down the stairwell.

Our youngest daughter was about three and she was coming up the stairs, about half way up. If she had been a few steps below, she would have been hit by it. But she was the blackest looking thing you ever saw. And of course she was terrified. You could just see the whites of her eyes.

Jean Drimmie,
Lang, Ontario

STRANDED

Once, I was supposed to be away for a week on the Magdalen Islands and I spent 30 days there. There was a heavy storm and the ice drifted in on the beach. We used to go down and look at it every day.

For 30 days we played cards in the hotel and sat around in the stores. There were 17 travellers there . . . eat and play cards. There was no liquor, because there wasn't any there, unless you found out where someone made homemade beer which wasn't very good; I never drank it. And every day we would go down and look at the ice.

There was always a lot of fun in the stores. Men would be sitting around eating out of the old cracker barrel. And they had pickled eggs, jars and jars of those at 5¢ a piece . . . and the fellows ate a lot of those. The eggs would be in vinegar, very, very good. And dried fish, smoked Digby herring. They made them in a smokehouse there and they'd eat the whole fish, head and all. With the pickled egg. Some lady made those for the store. Bologna. Crackers. Herrings. Eggs.

Every day we would go down and look at the ice and it was 25-30 feet high. A fisherman was down there with me one day and he said, "You'll be going out tomorrow."

I said, "What do you mean? There's 30 feet of ice there!"

He said, "It's gonna be gone."

"How do you know that?"

"Wind's gonna change. Gonna be south tomorrow and there's gonna be a storm and it will move that ice out."

And it was true. It drifted out and the sand there was as

hard as rock. Could hardly see the track of the old reliable DC3 when it arrived.

Gerald Nantes,
Magdalen Islands, Quebec

THE STRAW CURLING RINK

*T*hey built a curling rink beside the store . . . my dad started that too. Out of straw. They didn't have any lumber to build a curling rink, so they just built one up out of bales of straw. They put a small granary in front of it, that someone brought in, to do for an office. Everybody in the district co-operated. They hauled in straw. And they put poles on top and then covered it with straw. For light in there, they had kerosene lanterns, the kind you pump up, hung all along. They gave wonderful light.

So then the store became the in-between place. The curlers would wait in the store until it was time for them to curl. Back and forth. People would be watching the games and coming in and talking about who was ahead, what kind of shots were played.

Everybody curled then, kids, old people, young married couples. Bring their children in and put them in the back room of the store to sleep in there while they were curling. So the store was the centre. They'd sit around the stove and all around the store. A really good centre for community visiting: from 1936 on. That's what I can remember, the hustle and bustle of everybody coming and going, day and night.

Corine (McGarry) Stillborn,
Finnie, Saskatchewan

Most of the old stoves are gone today, but occasionally a new air-tight wood-burning stove moves into a country store. This one is in Lakehurst, Ontario.

144

CHAPTER ELEVEN

DEALING WITH THE DARK SIDE

The store is the place that has it all . . . all the beautiful things we covet and can't get. For a small boy this may be a jack-knife; for a wee girl, a marshmallow cookie; for a young man not making his own way well in the world, it may be the cash kept in the till.

Country stores across Canada have to deal with shoplifting and robberies, but in widely varying degree. In one area, the storekeeper rates all his customers as honest and says that strangers are not a problem. In another place . . . often on a main highway, near a railway station or a mainland ferry, providing quick get-aways . . . robberies are a fact of life.

The crimes vary from petty shoplifting to hold-ups by desperate, distorted people who will shoot to kill. Where stores are robbed by teens, alcohol is often involved. The kids are bored, drunk and looking for something reckless to do. For the storekeeper, break-ins and robberies are frustrating, unnerving and in some cases terrorizing.

But it is interesting how much tolerance and humour can appear in stories about being robbed, cheated or vandalized. Particularly in the case of young offenders, merchants are sometimes willing to forgive and forget and even to help. Perhaps this attitude is what keeps them sane in the face of a problem which can't be solved.

ONE A YEAR

We were broken into last night. No idea who did it. Another place was broken into in Borden and a service station in New Haven. They left the pinch bar in New Haven. Here they smashed the lock on my front door.

I have about one break-in a year. We had one big robbery: $8000. I never leave money in the till. That night I wrapped the money up, then said, "I think I'll go up to the club for a minute before I go home." I was only away for half an hour, came back and they had broken in and taken the money. They must have been watching me.

Prince Edward Island

CAUGHT IN THE COALSHED

We had robberies. We had everything else. I worked for George Marks and we had to do our own banking until they built the new bank in Carmangay. So then Mr. Marks went down one day to Carmangay and he had a week's "take" from the store in his buggy. And a guy came riding with a black horse and a big black hat and a kerchief over his face, to hold him up. Marks looked around and he seen that there was a team and rig coming back aways. So he kept stalling this guy and when they came up with him he told the driver what this guy was trying to do. And the robber he just turned and rode away.

So the next week, George says to me, "Harvey," he says, "you take our deposit today and use the big freighting wagon." So I took it and, sure enough, that guy stopped me in the same place. And a team and wagon came along and helped out that time. How that guy knew I had the money, we never could figure that one out. But he didn't get the money either time.

Then they tried to rob the store and the post office three or four times. Marks' homestead was a half mile north of town and he went out there at nights. I slept in the store at the back; we had a little kitchen where we'd get our meals there. And we had a big black dog, a stick-haired fellow called Bob. On in the night, this old dog let a growl out of him and he jumped right on the middle of me in bed.

I woke up. Here was a guy had pried the window up and he was half way through this window. I stood out of bed, I was gonna go around and jam the window down on him so he couldn't get away. But he spotted me and he got out of there. So I turned the dog out the door and I told him, "Take him, Bob." That guy, I think he ran into every piece of machinery in the yard and there was plenty of it there. He must have been black and blue.

Another night, we had a shipment of hardware, screen doors and stuff. We got it all into the store, but these screen doors. They were heavy . . . I think there were six of them in a bale. We set them up against a wall, didn't think anybody would bother them 'til morning. So I guess it would be about twelve, one o'clock. I heard a racket out there. I opened the door and headed out there. As luck would have it, old Bobby didn't stay with me that night.

Here he had just pried the crate loose and he had one door in his hands to go away with it. I walked up behind him and he didn't know I was there. And I told him, I said, "You'd better drop it!" Boy, he dropped the screen door and he pretty near broke his neck running.

But as time went on, we began to figure out who was doing a lot of it. We had a coalshed right beside the back door. And George says to me, "Harvey, that coal is going awful fast. We'll have to keep our eyes on it."

So sure enough, one night I heard this rustling in the coalbin and old Bobby raised up and he was growling. So I sneaked out and Bobby stayed on the bed and kept growling. And here it was the butcher and he had two of them big coal scuttles full of coal. I pulled the coalshed door shut and fastened it. There was no way he could get out from the inside. Oh, he begged, he did everything, but I never let on all night.

Next morning, George came down to the store. I was gettin' my breakfast and I said to him, "George," I said, "will you get a bucket of coal. I'm out of coal." He went out and opened the door and the butcher was sittin' on a coal bucket. He'd been sittin' there all night.

George, I thought he'd die laughing. He says to me, "How long has he been in there?"

I says, "Oh, from about midnight."

Harvey Beaubier,
Champion, Alberta

DAY AND NIGHT

*T*here were several robberies in Creston. I'm a light sleeper anyway, and this night this young couple have run out of gas up the hill here. We have an emergency gas can, but we ask for a deposit so the can comes back. So they scrounged up enough money for $6 worth of gas, which they put in the can, and they didn't have enough for the deposit, so the guy says, "Well, I'll leave my girlfriend."

So I looked out the window and my husband and the girl are standing out there. And the mosquitoes are atrocious. Fifteen minutes go by and they are still standing there. Another 15 minutes go by and I look out and he's saying, "Well, I think we'd better go sit inside." She's sort of giggling and making these squeaky kind of noises. I'm thinking, "Well, you never know, this day and age, the girls are crying rape and all, I better go down and see what's going on."

So I go tripping down, and finally the boyfriend and another guy shows up. What took them so long . . . the can has a spout, and if you loosen the top it pours real easy. They didn't know that, so they had poured every drop into a pop bottle first, then poured it into the van.

They are just about to leave when the police screech to a stop right in front of them. So the boy gets out and explains he'd run out of gas. (There had been a robbery in Creston at McDonald's and the police were out looking for suspects.)

Nickisch Shannon,
Sirdar, British Columbia

TWO ODD SHOES

*W*hen the Killick's store burned out, people stole so many shoes. There was an old warehouse where they piled all the stuff they had been able to save. And there was one man that had the nerve to come to the warehouse and try to mate up the shoes he had stolen. He had gotten two odd shoes.

Jenny Cony,
Rocky Mountain House, Alberta

◁ *This Vernon store south of Ottawa with its post office, horse collars and garden seeds is typical of the local store which had little protection against shoplifting or robbery. In rural areas almost everyone was known and trusted in the 1940s. Near large cities or on major highways, break-ins have become a problem.*

BEEF, IRON AND WINE

*T*here was a small detached Indian tribe that lived out west of Rocky Mountain House, called the Sunchild Indians. They originally belonged to the Chippewa tribe in the North. Some time in the period 150-200 years prior, they had had a series of terrible winters and had drifted down to the Rocky Mountain House area. And they were out of place because this was really Cree and Blackfoot country. But, as farming opened up in the area, they could pick roots for the clearing that was going on. And in the fall, they would be hired to stook the grain and help with the threshing.

Each family had a wagon pulled by a team of scrawny horses. The woman and a man would ride on the seat in front and have their kids in the back and a dog running under the wagon. The ladies wore coloured handkerchiefs around their heads, and they still wore Indian blankets and braids. The older men also braided their hair. The younger men would wear cowboy hats . . . they loved the whole cowboy scene.

In the summer, they would live in their tents on the fairground across the tracks. They would come into the store to shop and an Indian wife would choose a loaf of bread and put it on the counter. Then she'd turn around with her back to you and look into her purse and find the exact amount of money and turn around and give it to you. Then she would buy a pound of lard and repeat the same process. It was very, very time-consuming. None of them ever bought but one thing at a time, so one could spend hours selling $5 worth of groceries. However, amongst themselves they were very generous with their money; every child got a share of everything they had.

At that time there was an Interdiction List (everybody called it the Indian List) . . . Indians weren't allowed to drink alcoholic beverages and we weren't allowed to sell them vanilla or extracts of any kind as they had a high alcoholic content. We stayed open in the evening and in the fall it was dark after six o'clock. Some of the Indian guys had managed to get some booze during the day and on this occasion by seven o'clock they were pretty high. I kept a little drug section in my store and when I was new to the business, a very slick salesman had sold me two dozen quart bottles of *Beef, Iron and Wine* . . . it was a tonic you know and had a high percentage of alcohol . . . and I really had trouble getting rid of this darned stuff.

One day, a young brave came in . . . he was the chief's son, in his late '20s. As I waited on another customer, he was standing around talking and not making much sense. Suddenly, he stepped over by the drugs, reached up to the shelf and he grabbed two bottles of *Beef, Iron and Wine* and stuck them under his jacket and went roaring out the door.

I was on the wrong side of the counter, but I was young and agile, so I just leapfrogged over the counter and went after him. It was pitch-black outside and, as he crossed the road, I was about 20-25 feet behind him. Parked right across the road was a Model T Ford painted black. He was pretty loaded and he didn't notice it and he ran s-p-l-a-t right into that Model T Ford. Oh gosh, when I saw this it pulled me to a stop; my first thought was, ''Oh, he's killed himself!'' But he slithered along the car and somehow got around the back of the car and away he went down the hill in the dark. I don't know how he survived the collision. I know he kept his *Beef, Iron and Wine* and he didn't break the bottles.

I assume he drank it and I hope he enjoyed it. It had a horrible flavour . . . about like drinking rust.

Don Wilkes,
Benalto, Alberta

Trusted neighbours and a comfortable community surround most country stores, but occasionally good roads or railways or ferries bring transients and trouble.

BROKEN WINDOWS

I remember when they had a big fire in Greenwood and the heat from the fire broke all the windows in the liquor store. So, as one bunch of men fought the fire, another bunch of fellows went and got all the liquor they could haul and they took it to Johnny Meyers barn, and the whole town went on a drunk for days and days.

The next time there was a real big fire . . . from Brown's Store, the whole block burned . . . the first thing they did was go down and break the windows in the liquor store and get the liquor again for another big drunk.

I remember we kids went into Brown's Store and we had loads of boxes of chocolates, and it was deep snow on the road and we were piling them in the snow to keep the fire from melting them. And we got them away and got them hid. But the police made us take every damn one of them back the next day. It was terrible; never got away with nothing.

Kay Jones,
Greenwood, British Columbia

WAITING IN THE HOUSE FOR ME

I've had quite a few break-ins, about five in the last 10 years. Once I had a guy waiting in the house for me. He was hiding behind the oil burner there to hit me over the head when I came in with the money. My mother was with me then and she was in the house, gone to sleep already when it happened. When I came in, she said somebody had been in the house, hiding behind the heater. She couldn't get out of bed, her legs weren't good, but she was not that easy to scare . . . a good woman, but not that easy to scare.

Then I heard the trees rustle outside, so I locked the house so Mother was safe in the house, and there was a car hanging around so I knew the driver and told him to give me a ride a little ways south, and then I circled back to the store and phoned the police.

About half an hour later the police were here, parked west of the store, and we saw these guys pulling the window off. So we let them crawl in the window and then the police came in and got them. So after that I rigged up a burglar alarm.

Stefan Stefanson,
Hnausa, Manitoba

WITH A CAN OF DOG FOOD

We've had two robberies. I never hear a thing at night myself, but the wife, she wakes me up. "Joe, there's somebody downstairs in the store." So the first time I go down half asleep and the window is broken out in the door, and the robbers are gone. But the police caught them half way to Peterborough.

The second time, my wife wakes me up again. I come downstairs and the glass is broken in the door again, and in the dark I can make out this guy coming in. I say to my wife, "You phone the police, I'll stay here." So I throw a couple of cans of dog food at him and I hit him in the side. He yells, "Hold it Joe! Stop it! It's me . . . Mike!" It was a local boy.

I busted my own window too. With the first can, I missed.

But I feel sorry for that kid, really I do. His mom and dad broke up. And he was out with a gang that dared him to do a thing like this. And now he's got a police record.

With somebody you don't know, you don't care that much. But it's different if you know the kid. And it cost him $500 . . . including the windows.

Ontario

GUILTY BY HIS TRACKS

In our Cape Negro store, we used to have these great big wooden tierces of molasses, about five barrels in size. We kept this out in the shed and we didn't lock the shed. There was a poor family a mile or so from us and they had a boy. He used to come in the evening to visit us Ross kids. There wasn't that much to do in Cape Negro in the wintertime, and we always had funny papers he could read.

His mother would give him a lard pail and he'd quietly put it under the molasses tierce, then come in and visit us. Of course, molasses runs very slowly in the wintertime.

But one night, it was very warm when he was doing this.

And that night my mother was making fudge. So he stayed longer then he was supposed to.

This molasses ran all over the floor. He went out, stepped in the molasses and took the overloaded pail. When we got up in the morning, here were these tracks of molasses and this trail of molasses going all along the bank and down the road in the snow to his house.

My mother sent for his mother and made out that she was very annoyed.

Joseph Ross,
Cape Negro, Nova Scotia

THEY SURE PAID WELL

The chap who ran this store used to have a store down at Pekokie in southeastern Alberta, and it was on the road for all the whiskey travellers and they used to have big Studebaker cars going from Montana up to Medicine Hat. They used to wake him up . . . he wouldn't know which night . . . they'd arrive about three or four in the night with their big cars, and wake him up because they needed gasoline to get back into the States.

He said he ne-v-er questioned them because they were a pretty rough bunch. But he said he never turned them in either because they sure paid well.

Don Mallory,
Kirkcaldy, Alberta

BLACK PEPPER FOR A BLIND PIG

There were two brothers who staked a property in Quebec in 1922. They wanted so much for their claims that no mining company would buy them. Of course, a prospector, if he doesn't sell, is not making any money to live on.

Anyway, these two came to Cheminis on the Ontario-Quebec border and built a good-sized, rough-board shack on the Ontario side, and made chairs and tables out of rough lumber. As a kid, I was wondering what they were going to do. I had an inkling it was going to be a blind pig . . . bootlegging!

It was Prohibition time in Ontario. And you see, there was a payday at Cheminis every day during the building of the railway. The crew that were doing the blasting would be paid on Monday, the one doing the grading be paid on Tuesday, the one building the bridge on Wednesday, the one working in the cookhouse on Thursday. With the railway there, they could get all the beer they wanted from Quebec. They would address it to "Cheminis, Ontario, Dassarat Township, Quebec". And the Ontario Provincial Police couldn't hold that beer. It would be delivered onto the Quebec side. They had a cache there and whenever they needed a bit, they would bring it back over the border.

Anyway, these two brothers used to come into the store and they would order five pounds of black pepper. Black pepper used to come in a wooden box. Every once in a while, they would say, "Get me five pounds of black pepper." We began to wonder why they would want all that black pepper, two fellows alone, batching it.

We found out what they were doing with it. In the shack there would be all these different nationalities drinking in there, maybe 50 or 60 people drinking beer, and things would get out of hand. Then they'd start to fight. All they had for light was a coal-oil lamp and, with the men smoking, the air would be blue with smoke and it would be sort of dark. So when these two bootleggers would notice that there was going to be trouble, they would put the black pepper into a tall can of baking powder, then pour some into pepper shakers. They would take two of these and go along and shake them where the arguments were breaking out.

Then the men would start to sneeze and they would have to get up and go out and get their second breath. So there wouldn't be any fight.

Albert Emond,
Cheminis, Ontario

THE DEVIL'S OWN STORE

*T*he man who built our stone house in Port Hood was a store-keeper named Smythe who was a millionaire, but he was a devil. He came here in 1818 and went into partnership with Flynn, so the store was always called Smythe and Flynn, but I don't know what became of Flynn. Smythe kept a big barrel of rum in his store and let his customers help themselves. He encouraged them to drink too much and to buy too much. Then when they were in debt to him, he foreclosed on their farms.

Before Smythe died, they said, he could walk on his own land all the way from Port Hood to the Canso Causeway.

Joyce McCulloch,
Port Hood, Nova Scotia

I WATCHED THEM DRIVE AWAY

*T*his robbery happened right in plain daylight. Oh, we were so mad about that! There were two men and a lady came in, and we should have caught on that they were different. They were looking at the seeds and gardening stuff and didn't buy any, but said they'd be back. Well, they get the joint pretty well looked over. We had a McCaskey (a small cash safe) down near the back where we kept our extra money, and one of the men was watching that.

After dinner they came back. Bruce was in the office, and they got me over on the dry goods side looking at jeans, while one chap stayed over by the McCaskey. When I look back on it now, I remember that I saw him give the others just a little nod.

So, later when the bread man came in, we went to get the money and pay him and — No Money! And all our Shin Plasters (small bills, now collectors' items) gone too. We had a leather folder we kept the money in and we kept that in a drawer of the McCaskey; he had just quietly opened it. And I stood in the door and watched them drive away . . . said good-bye to my money.

When we called the police, they said, "Did you happen to have two men and a lady in?" They had done it in other places. But they never caught them.

After Bruce died, I used to be just terrified staying alone in that great big place. I stayed at my sister's two or three nights, then I thought, well, I can't do this. I've got to start sometime. But I'd hear all these noises, hear a car at the front and get up and look out around to see what was going on. I'd hear every sound!

Helen Ryley,
Bethany, Ontario

CHAPTER TWELVE

WHOLESALERS AND TRAVELLIN' MEN

They were not your average stay-at-home nine-to-five workers. To survive, they needed a sense of adventure and a tough resilience. In a cold country subject to violent weather, it was no easy matter to call on 50-100 country stores every two weeks. It involved getting lost on wrong roads, stuck in mud, caught in floods; it involved the risk of an accident on the road or of freezing to death in a storm. Old Bert Carman had to scale mountains. Gerry Nantes had to face open Atlantic seas in fair weather or foul. But, as Kenn Gadd tells us, there was fun as well; where two or three travellers got together, they made sure there was.

Travelling salesmen were essential to the operation of a country store. They took the orders, introduced new products, dealt with dissatisfaction and brought in news of the wide world. Most travellers were admired and respected by the storekeepers. Older ones took on an almost legendary quality, particularly in remote areas. Younger ones were looked after by motherly storekeepers who fed them or provided them with stopping places. Many of them acquired nicknames from their merchants . . . Big Tiny Little, Red Sam McGregor, Give-Away Coutes, Sunny Jim . . . according to their size, shape or

This was the Ballinafad stage in front of the Ballinafad, Ontario store. The two-seater democrat carried mail until 1925. (from Tweedsmuir History, Silverwood, Women's Institute)

characteristics, or things that had happened to them on the road.

Canada's old-time travellers were an aggressive but benevolent army, traipsing over a vast land from Newfoundland to Vancouver Island and into the frozen north, selling from sea to shining sea with a great spirit of humour and fun. Many of them genuinely loved the land they trod. They deserve to be remembered.

SUNNY JIM ROSS

*T*here would usually be two travellers and they would hire a team of horses in Baddeck and go right up to Cape North, 80 or 85 miles, then turn around and come back.

Sunny Jim Ross was a favourite. He never got a car, always travelled by horse and buggy until he died. He would have a driver. He was quite a gentleman, a big stout, fine-looking man. He would stay at our old home and he liked service, liked to be catered to. He always watched out for the weather. If it looked stormy, he wouldn't move.

He travelled for a grocery firm, Tobins in Halifax. They specialized in Tobins Orange Pekoe Tea. We would buy a 100-pound chest and sell it by the pound. We would have two or three chests at one time. Sunny Jim would take the orders and it would come in by ship.

His home was up the Annapolis Valley; every two weeks he'd get home. But I believe he died in some hotel, still in the harness. That was his life. He was a great fellow for the job. People liked to see him coming.

A.J. and Jessie Morrison,
North River Bridge, Nova Scotia

GIVE-AWAY COUTES

*W*e had four or five biscuit travellers and there were seven different bread men at one time. Benny Hans was quite a character. And we had Jake Fritz. One morning Benny Hans came in and right after him, Jake Fritz. So we had Hans and Fritz . . . the funny papers, the Katzenjammer Kids.

We had Jim Webster, a Swifts' traveller, a great big fellow, from Cranbrook. And there was Jim Coutes. I knew Coutes when I worked in Cranbrook; he worked in J.B. McBride's hardware store. You'd go in for a pocket knife. ''$1.25. Oh, just give me two bits.'' And he soon got the name of Give-away Coutes.

So he lost his job there and he got on travelling for different dry-goods people. He didn't have a car, he'd have to bum rides with other travellers. So this particular day, he asked Jim Webster if he could go down to Creston with him. Jim said,

Ballinafad store as it looks today.

159

"Yes, providing you leave the empty suitcase at home."

Jim was telling me that Coutes would have several suitcases for dry goods. He would go into a store and open up his suitcase and the storekeeper would have to leave him to wait on a customer, and by the time Coutes was through in that store, he would have stuff in his empty suitcase. That was his method of doing business, taking that empty suitcase out in the morning and bringing it home full. He didn't last long at one job. Changed very often.

British Columbia

OLD BERT CARMAN OF McKAY SMITH BLAIR

*T*he lodge rooms over the Pavilion store were filled with transients; the store was a stopping place for commercial travellers. Old Bert Carman was the traveller for McKay Smith Blair, a dry-goods salesman. He used to travel on the stage coaches . . . four horses maybe . . . through these mountains. They would put heated-up rocks in the coach to keep their feet warm, and bear skins around them. Sometimes they got to places where they'd be all stretched out in the living room, keeping the fires going. It used to get very, very cold, north of Clinton, in that area.

He would have a showroom in the hotel. All the storekeepers would go to see his stuff laid out. In the summer, he'd have a showroom for the fall stuff. He had all these heavy plaid shirts, woollen stuff, mackinaws. He had a line called Pride of the West which was the competitor of G.W.G., the Alberta one.

John Moss,
Pavilion, British Columbia

WHOLESALE FRIENDS

*O*ur store was a boarding house, too. A Mr. Stevenson stayed here about once a month for 17 years. He travelled from St. John's, but he would go all over Newfoundland. Worked for Halley & Company Dry Goods, then for Kaufman Rubber.

In later years, he used to bring his wife. She used to come upstairs and bake cookies for me. She would say, "You go on and do your store work and I'll do the cookin'."

And when I would go up to St. John's on business, Mr. Stevenson would pick me up at whatever store I was shopping at, and he would bring me home to have my dinner with them.

Ralph Lefitz was another traveller who liked to come here. I had a maid then and she used to cook up cabbage and beef and potatoes and pudding . . . a Newfie dinner, he'd call it. He would let us know when he'd be coming and she would have a big feed cooked. He'd sooner eat the dinner than sell the goods.

Muriel Palfrey,
Placentia, Newfoundland

FINE TIME

*T*ravellers would come out from St. John's and they'd have a few bottles of rum. It was kind of a trade-drawer. It would get you buying good. Hell of a fine time when they came!

Some were gamblers, too. Set up a poker game. But a lot of the storekeepers were good poker players too. Sometimes the storekeepers would rip off the smart guys from St. John's.

Gus Hayes,
Stephenville, Newfoundland

Large stores, such as this one in Ennismore, Ontario, led double lives. "It was a hotel in the days when there were floating bridges. The travellers, they just had a horse and buggy or sleigh and they would come from Peterborough across the Chemong Lake Floating Bridge, show their wares and stay overnight, then in daylight, go across the Pigeon Creek Floating Bridge to Bobcaygeon."

THE ONLY DISHONEST TRAVELLER I EVER MET

I'd been missing certain things in the store for a long time and I was blaming the children. Then I got suspicious of a certain traveller. When he came into the store, he'd go and check my smallwares. So I left word with the staff that if he came in, and I was not in the store, to count the ball-point pens and things. So when I came back, they told me how many there were. And he came and said, "Mr. Stillborn, you need some ball-point pens. I've got a special on."

I said, "I've got pens there."

"Oh," he said, "you've only got one pen."

What he'd done, he'd taken all the pens out the back. Nobody else had been in the store. I never let him in again and I warned the other merchants around. The only dishonest traveller I ever met.

Another traveller came in that day and wanted to go check the soap. I said, "I don't know whether I'll let you in or not." So I told him. And oh, he was cross. He went to Regina that night and checked, but the fellow didn't belong to the Travellers Association, or they would have stepped on him.

Herbie Stillborn,
Duff, Saskatchewan

NEW SHOES

*N*elson Ghan is one of these salty old wholesalers who dealt with the salty old grocers. He's a good friend of ours now, and he says the first time he met Wally he could tell he was nervous about the meeting because he had on new shoes. He has never seen Wally with new shoes on since.

What he said to him . . . he stood Wally up and said, "What the hell makes you think you can run a grocery store?" Wally had left the Air Force and wanted to get into business. He came back and told me about *that man.*

That terrible man! Looked over the top of his glasses at me. But was he a help to me after? Absolutely! He was one of those people . . . of which there are many in the grocery business, who really want to help, not from a monetary standpoint but just because they like the business; they like people, and they understand their job. We got a lot of help from that. It's still possible for a beginner because there are still people like that around.

Carla and Wally Protsack,
Rocky Mountain House, Alberta

THEY HAD TO FLY IN

You don't see country salesmen like they used to be. They were extroverts. Especially over on Vancouver Island, where they had to fly in . . . and they'd get together to fly in. That's when we would really have fun. We storekeepers would switch their products in the suitcases. One fellow would have all different cookies to show people, so we'd get someone else's products and put them in. So when he'd get to the next place and open up his suitcase, he would have someone else's products in it.

Evelyn Jackson,
Port Hardy, British Columbia

HOW'S YOUR UNDERWEAR?

Between Mother and the wholesalers, there existed a certain bond of camaraderie and understanding. I think, to her, they represented the larger world out there. Personally, I liked the one who always came in saying, "How's your underwear, Mrs. Swerdfeger?" He really did sell Stanfield underwear. But his entrance never failed to topple us kids off the dry-goods counter and send us bolting out in a fit of snickers.

Enid Swerdfeger,
Glen Stewart, Ontario

A NICE BARGAIN

Around 1925 or 1926, the railway hadn't reached Noranda; Cheminis was still the end of the line. There was this chap who had a dry-good store at Rouyn, near Noranda. We used to see him come back and forth by stage to the railway. Then I think he went bankrupt.

Some of the signs with which travellers adorned country stores, are now collectors items.

One day just about train time, the stage came in and he was on it. In the excitement of the train coming and leaving, the store would be quite busy. So this fellow came to my father with a great big box and he said, "You want to buy all these rubbers?" He said he had so many pairs of rubber boots.

Dad was busy, people coming in and out, the train coming. This fellow was in a hurry and my dad was in a hurry. So the man said what he wanted and it was a nice bargain, so Dad bought them.

After everything quieted down, Dad said to me, "Pair those rubbers up and put them on the shelf for sale."

There were 10 or 12 pair. But they were all left feet! They were all samples he got from the manufacturer. Anytime he bought a different kind of rubber, the traveller had given him a sample and the sample was always for thc lcft foot.

Of course he was on the train to Toronto. And he was never coming back.

Albert Emond,
Cheminis, Ontario

GETTING TO THE STORE ALIVE

*T*he company I represented was DeBloise Brothers, wholesale groceries . . . headquarters in Charlottetown. I started travelling for them in 1940.

At that time, we would go by car in summertime. In winter, it would be by car, train, horse and sleigh around Prince Edward Island. I also travelled on the Magdalen Islands and to get there we would fly or go by boat.

It was a cruel place, when you got there first. I arrived there in April 1940, dressed in spat rubbers and a light coat, thought I would be landing at an airport. Nobody told me. The boss didn't know much about it either. I landed on the beach. Not a building anywhere. I near froze standing there.

Somebody said, "Have you got a drive? Well, you can't walk, it's five miles!" A local person, who came for a passenger in a jog cart, said he would send somebody down from Grindstone. So eventually a fellow came with a little cart, two wheels on it; and he took me and my suitcase and grip up to a hotel in Grindstone. After that I would always make arrangements to be met.

There were 1200 people on the Islands. It would take me a week or 10 days to visit the 55 stores. After I got their orders, the service boat would bring the groceries. I would get there every three months during spring, summer and fall, but there was no connection at all in the winter. In the fall, Island stores would get in enough to last them until spring.

In the spring, we travelled by horse and sleigh on the ice. Or by dog-team. I would go across to Grande-Entrée, another little island which had eight or ten stores. It was 40 miles from Grindstone if you went by the beach . . . it was more or less connected to land by sandbars . . . but only 15 miles across by water. We'd go across the ice until about the end of March. Sometimes the priest, Father Nadeau, would take me with his team of six dogs. Or we would go by horse and sleigh. They carried poles on the sides of the sleigh for tapping the ice in the spring. We had a horse go in one time. The horse stopped, but the driver thought the ice was good and made him go, hit him with a whip. And the horse went in. But we got him out.

There were no roads on the Magdalen Islands and only three or four cars. In summer, we would drive on the beach when the tide was out. There was one place we would cross about 400 yards where the tide never went very low, always a foot or so of water. So we'd take the fan belt off the car and drive across. One night we got stuck there in the sand and the tide was coming in.

The driver told me there would be somebody come along, but we waited for a long time. And the tide came in pretty fast there. It was soon up on the car, so we thought we would start walking. I was carrying my grip which had between eight and ten thousand dollars in it.

I started to wade . . . I couldn't swim very much . . . it was up to my waist and I couldn't do it. So we went back and waited on top of the car. He assured me it wouldn't go over it. It came up about six inches from the top. It was getting dark.

But the people in Grindstone knew we should have been back. There was a policeman and he came out with an amphibian and took us off.

Next day, he went out again with the amphibian, after the tide went out, and hauled out the car. We rinsed out the salt, put rugs over the seats and were driving it the next day.

One September night, we had to cross on a boat from Grande-Entrée. And it was a wicked night. My driver was

Fabiane Arsenault, a fisherman, and he told me, "There's gonna be a storm. We've got to get out of here no later than three o'clock."

So I was ready at three o'clock. After we got out of the narrows, the storm struck. Out on the ocean in a 38-foot fishing boat. There were 40-foot waves. He had lots of gas and we were tied in, in case we'd go over. My job was to put the gas in, and if you've ever tried to put gas out of a puncheon into a bucket, and tried to get it through a funnel and it blowin' in the air . . .!

We put a kind of shield of traps up, and I would face myself to that and I'd pour it in. He was fighting into the wind and we were going back more than we were going forward. He kept telling me there was no danger. He kept us pointed into the wind. We left at three in the afternoon and the trip should have taken four hours. We got in at four o'clock in the morning.

House Harbour was the place we came into. Everybody was out looking for us. We didn't go in to the wharf because it was too rough. We landed on a beach, but couldn't go in close because we didn't want the boat to hit bottom. We anchored the boat. He was a great hefty guy and he jumped into the water. He had a long rope with an anchor and he'd throw another anchor ahead. We'd hold onto the rope and when we'd get to the anchor, he would throw it again. You couldn't stand in the water alone because it was too rough. We covered about 500 feet, pulling ourselves in by that rope. There were people waiting on the beach for us, to give us a hot drink of coffee and rum, and take us up to the house and give us dry clothes.

Gerald Nantes,
Magdalen Islands, Quebec

THE FUN OF IT

*B*ancroft was a staging area for travellers. This was right after the Second World War. We'd all stay at the Bancroft Hotel. The train that ran west through Highland Grove and Wilberforce would be loaded with travellers, sometimes 20 or 25 travellers on that train. We'd all get on at eight o'clock in the morning and go chugging out there, and, when we'd arrive at a station, the business people would come down to the station and business would be done right there. Some travellers would leave off a price list and stop off again on the way back to pick up the order. The train would come through only once a week.

When we went east from Bancroft, we'd join together in a car. Quaker had two salesmen; one sold feed and I was the grocery products guy, and we'd take along a wholesale salesman from George Robertson in Kingston. We'd go out this country road to an area they called The Horn . . . it was shaped like a horn and you'd go out one way and back around the other way. We'd leave at daybreak and make seven or eight calls in a day, and we'd all go in and call on the storekeeper together. They were all country general stores . . . McArthur's Mills, Hermon, Boulter. We'd agree who would make the sales pitch first and the others would wait.

We'd have dinner at one of the stores. We'd pay for it, and the woman would serve us dinner. The last call we'd make would be Tom Turff's at L'Amable about 20 miles from Bancroft. We'd get in there about 10 o'clock at night, and we'd bring out a bottle and end up back at the Bancroft Hotel about one o'clock at night.

One day, we were coming up to one store and the guys looked at their watches and said, "Golly. We'll be just in time for the Prayer Meeting." They started telling me that this gal in the store was very, very religious, and if she was having a prayer meeting, she'd expect us to join her, probably sing a hymn or two and have prayer, right in the general store. And any customers in there would join in too.

They said, "Whatever you do, Gadd, clean up your act. And don't swear!" I was the youngest of the three of us. So as we got closer and closer, I was straightening my tie and making sure I was just right.

So the three of us walked in through the front door, and she looks up . . . "Well, I'll be God Damned. Where have you Sons of Bitches been, anyway!"

And that was the prayer meeting. She had the foulest mouth you'd ever hear, although she was really a nice person. The two of them had made up the prayer meeting and they had me really on edge to behave myself.

Ken Gadd,
Peterborough, Ontario

A TRAVELLER'S STORM

I got stuck on the other side of Souris and had a Canada Packers traveller with me, who thought he had a heart condition and wouldn't get out of the car. He wanted us to stay there. We stayed from about three o'clock in the afternoon until about eleven o'clock at night. The car started covering over. We couldn't have the motor on. He complained terrible, didn't want me to go.

I said, "You're gonna die here alone. I'm going to go for help." I could see a light and I started walking through the snow so high I was rolling. When I got pretty close to this house, the lights went out.

But when I rapped on the door, the man knew me. He put his head out the upstairs window and said, "Is that you, Gerry? We've been watching for you from six o'clock. Everybody has been phoning." The telephone operators would have some idea where I was and they would phone around.

So he came down and got out a horse and sleigh. The horse floundered badly in the snow. By this time, though, there was a fellow coming with a plough, a big turner-dozer with wide wheels, and he was looking for us. When we got back to the truck, the Canada Packers fellow was O.K., but he was so excited that he didn't know me.

Gerald Nantes,
Charlottetown, Prince Edward Island

STRANDED

*Q*uaker Oats salesmen always drove Chevies, and in the 1940s the auto industry didn't know how to make a heater. Oh, we had heaters by this time, but they weren't worth a damn. I had been in the Air Force during the war and I came out with heavy fleece-lined boots and I always wore them. And a heavy overcoat and long underwear and mitts. You would never drive bare-handed.

Alec Willis was a Quaker feed salesman. One time he was travelling in northern Ontario, and he got caught in freezing rain and didn't have chains with him. He got in a valley between two hills, in the bottom of an icy saucer.

It was late afternoon and cold, and he had no way of getting out. So he gathered up firewood and lit a large bonfire right beside the car, on the side away from the gas tank. With the car door open, he curled up on the front seat . . . I don't know how because he was a big man about six-foot-four, but he let his feet hang out the door by the fire so they didn't freeze. Through the night he would wake up and keep the fires going. So he survived.

Ken Gadd,
Peterborough, Ontario

AUNT JEMIMA

Quaker sold Aunt Jemima Pancake Flour. It originated in the last century, around 1892. Quaker didn't own it at first, but bought it before the turn of the century. I used to take Aunt Jemima around and we'd call on a grocer and arrange a demonstration in a store, and we'd be there on a certain day and we'd bring in the griddles and mix up the batter and we'd serve pancakes. The store would advertise beforehand in the local paper.

We had a coloured girl named Vera Marshall and she was so much fun, played the piano beautifully and sang. She would stand there and cook the pancakes and flip them and chuckle and laugh and have a lot of fun. Quaker got away from this, because in Chicago the Association for the Rights of Coloured People demonstrated in front of a store where they were having an Aunt Jemima demonstration. This seems pretty narrow-minded, because she was a national figure and very popular. But Quaker got rid of all their Aunt Jemima pancake houses, and Aunt Jemima is now getting whiter and whiter on the package.

For these demonstrations, I used to decorate the stores with Aunt Jemima packages, and we had little Aunt Jemima and Uncle Moses salt and pepper shakers, and rag dolls which we would give away. For syrup on the pancakes, we used to tie in with St. Lawrence Crown Brand Corn Syrup. And, in later years, Quaker put out its own brand of Aunt Jemima syrup.

We also put on pancake suppers. In a small community, the storekeeper was usually involved with the church, so he would say, "Would you come and do a pancake supper?" Quaker would donate the pancake flour and we would have the grill,

and I'd get Aunt Jemima and we'd go down in the church basement and mix up great batches of batter. We'd get the griddle heated and throw out dozens of pancakes until we got them just right. Then the people would come and the church would make money.

We did it for nothing. I enjoyed doing it. It was overtime work and we didn't get paid for it. Not like today. But it was fun.

Ken Gadd,
Peterborough, Ontario

Travellers still take orders, and vans still deliver the goods. This is the Cherry Valley store in Ontario's Prince Edward County.

SELLING CHRISTMAS CAKE TO MILLIE

I called on the stores and I called on the public along the roads, too. I had an Indian lady on my route, back near Nogies Creek. She was very, very close with her money. Millie, her husband and her husband's brother lived together. She would phone the store at Nogies Creek for me to bring her groceries. She would have her money for groceries in one stocking, her husband's money for tobacco in another stocking and her brother-in-law's money in another. And the storekeeper, his name was Junkin, bet me $5 one day that I couldn't sell Millie a Christmas cake. He said, "If you can, you should be selling refrigerators to Eskimos."

So, of course, anything damaged you were allowed to sell it cheaper. So I broke the end off this Christmas cake and I sold Millie the cake.

I didn't hold the storekeeper to his bet. $5 was too hard to come by then. But Millie died a wealthy woman. When they took the wallpaper off the walls, there was money stuck all over the house under the wallpaper. Her husband and his brother were both guides on Pigeon Lake and she did sewing and knitting, and they spent nothing.

They had an old Model T Ford with the little brass radiator and carbon lights. It sat in the garage and the farthest it ever went was from Nogies Creek to Bobcaygeon (five miles). It was to Peterborough once (30 miles). The Ford Motor Company offered them a new car, I couldn't say what year that was. But they wouldn't take it.

Instead of driving the car to Nogies Creek for groceries, she phoned for me to bring them out. I could depend on it three times a week.

Earl Mark,
Lindsay, Ontario

WHEN I ATE THE DOG FOOD

*O*ne of the new Quaker products we introduced was Kennel Ration. At that time, we made the only good dog food there was, and to prove it was good, we'd open a can and eat a bit right in the store. My area included stores in Toronto, and there was one little store on Parliament Street that was really dirty. It had a horrible odour. When I ate the dog food in that store, I almost threw up.

Ken Gadd,
Peterborough, Ontario

WITH THE WIDOW

Remember the time I stayed with Mrs. Hynes. I was coming from Montague and couldn't see a foot ahead of me. So I pulled into her driveway and she made me stay all night. She was a widow.

I was only there about a half hour when the lights went out. We played cards by candlelight. The storm eased up about 11 o'clock, and my car was facing into the wind from the north and it was terrible. So I said, "I think I'll go out and start my car and face it out toward the road." Which I did . . . my car started. But I was only back in the house a minute when her phone started ringing. It was the neighbours who had seen me and wanted to know was there something wrong.

She was a good sport. She said, "Just mind your own business, I've got a man here and it's none of your business."

Gerald Nantes,
Charlottetown, Prince Edward Island

CHAPTER THIRTEEN

JACK-OF-ALL-TRADE:

From the beginning, Canada's typical storekeeper has been a jack-of-all-trades. Dicky Paul Anderson, the first storekeeper at Glen Stewart, made coffins in a shed behind the store in the 1800s. Herman Kavelman of New Dundee, Ontario pulled teeth for his customers. Gordon Shears in Rocky Harbour, Newfoundland built 98 boats. Walter Cameron in Fallbrook, Ontario shod the farmer's horses; while Isobel Cameron sold dry goods and groceries to the farmer's wife.

Countless storekeepers dealt in lumber, coal, stove-wood, cedar rails, fish, furs, potatoes, flour, feed, seed grain and farm machinery. In Phillipsville, Ontario, the store of R.J. Taylor shipped quantities of maple syrup each spring. John Moss of Pavilion, British Columbia ran a resort around his store, rented cabins and seven rooms above the store. Edna Stabler put a coffee table in their Brant, Alberta store, while her husband added a barber shop. More than a few merchants had extensive barns and sheds to accommodate the horses, cows, pigs and goats taken in barter. Milton Swerdfeger at Glen Stewart was killing his own pigs in the 1940s by the barn behind his store. In a store at Mountain Station, before he moved to Glen Stewart, he dug horse-radish from his lot and shipped five or six bags a day via the railway opposite his store.

For 150 years, the country store in Canada has been the most adaptable of institutions. While so many cheese factories, blacksmith shops and mills, rural hotels, schools and churches have disappeared off the face of Canada, the country store stays on, often drastically changed from its early self, but still finding a way to serve the public and survive.

Flexibility kept many a merchant afloat when the times were rough. If the bottom dropped out of the feed or dry-goods business, he tried cordwood or farm machinery, or sold livestock or Model T cars.

This same flexibility made entrepreneurs out of the most imaginative when the times were good. Ralph S. Allison, in the tiny village of Winchester Springs, Ontario, bought a bankrupt general store in the 1930s. Eventually, he bought a truck to cart feed to his feedstore. He expanded his trucking business, and today his son, Lloyd, operates a fleet of transport trucks out of Winchester Springs.

Joseph Shepard built his store in 1860 in a flourishing part of York County where Sheppard Avenue now crosses Yonge Street in Toronto. By 1870, his son, Joseph, was postmaster, merchant and owner of prosperous flour and lumber mills.

Flexibility and imagination did occasionally make millionaires. Timothy Eaton comes to mind, starting out in his dry-goods store in the village of St. Marys, Ontario in the 1860s. Timothy had a radical belief that barter was on its way out, that even in rural areas people would be able to pay cash for goods with a money-back guarantee. Twenty years later his Eaton's catalogue was almost a family member in homes from coast to coast.

Storekeepers in remote areas have often been called upon to perform services for which they had no training and even less liking. They pulled teeth and cut hair. They transported expectant mothers to hospital and, if that were too slow, they delivered babies. They got involved in politics, became Justices of the Peace, captured criminals, portaged sick or dead men out to civilization.

Variety was the spice of their lives, and most of them thrived on it. Few country storekeepers got ulcers or took heart attacks. An amazing number of them are still hale and hearty in their 80s or 90s.

Early storekeepers, like these two in British Columbia, had to do for themselves, whatever needed to be done.

TO MAKE ENDS MEET

*T*his storekeeper, Anton Jaworski, was a man of many talents, and in order to make ends meet during the '30s, he became a jack-of-all-trades. He helped to build houses and assisted in building the community hall and the local Ukrainian church. In his small woodworking shop, he patiently carved and sanded the furnishings for the church, visiting churches and supply houses in the city to get measurements and ideas.

He could repair harness, or resole your shoes. One son would give you a haircut; or they would replace a broken window pane. They had a garden and kept pigs, cows and chickens. For several years they had a threshing outfit and did threshing for some of the local farmers.

And if a customer pounded on the store door at 2 a.m. for some "Kobasa" to go with the beer at a party, someone would open up to see what he wanted.

Walter Dziadow,
Arborg, Manitoba

THE FERRY AND THE FARMERS' LINE

*A*cross from the Hatfield store, we operated a wire ferry that went across the St. John River here. It could carry a double team and a single rig at once. There would be loads of potatoes going over steady in the fall. Fifty cents for a double team over and back. Five cents a foot passenger at first, then it went up to 10¢.

For its power, the ferry just used the river current. There were sideboards and a set of blocks, and they could set the sideboards to catch the current. And the wire up above had pulleys on it. Father would send my brother and I out to run it a lot. Travellers would stand on the far shore and holler, "Over! Over! Over!"

Grandfather Hatfield started the post office here. He got $100 a year for running it and taking the mail across on the ferry to catch the train. The train would go through to the north between twelve and one o'clock noon. On the other side, they would hang the mail on a pole with an arm on it; the railway's mail car had a mechanical arm that would come out and grab the bag of mail and never have to stop.

In the wintertime, the ferry didn't run because, in those days, the ice would freeze solid. One year in the spring, an ice jam came down and broke the wire that held the ferry. Dad had a hard job getting that wire up there again, and he just got it fixed when a jam of logs came down and broke it again.

And just downstream, the Farmers' Telephone Company had all their wires going across the river. Well, the logs carried the ferry and its cable down and broke all the telephone wires.

The Farmers' Line Company tried to sue us for it. We wouldn't pay, so we were taken to court, and the judge ruled that Dad's cable ferry had the right-of-way because it was there long before the telephone line.

But Farmers' Line came and took our phone out of the store and for three years we had no telephone. When we finally did get one, we had to put it in the house under our name, not Father's.

Harry Hatfield,
Simonds, New Brunswick

THE SCHOOL CABOOSE

*M*y wife kept the store, while I drove a school caboose. The school west of Broad Valley had only about half a dozen pupils, so they decided to close it and cart the children to town. This was in 1930. So I drove them in a car in the summertime and, in the wintertime up until Christmas, I hauled by team of horses with six or seven kids in the little caboose. In January and February, they closed the school for two months.

We would start off about six o'clock in the morning; it took about three hours to make the trip. It was a closed-in caboose built onto a cutter, so they were sheltered, out of the wind. They dressed warmly, and when you go west from here there was still a lot of bush and you were sheltered by that.

Myroslaw Tretiak,
Broad Valley, Manitoba

THE LOBLAWS BOAT

*F*rom the store at Young's Point, we ran what we called the Loblaws Boat. We bought the store in 1934 and started the boat the second year. We'd have places to stop on Stony Lake and they would come from all the different islands. And they loved it; they'd have a real gossip.

The first time after we were married that we made any money was on that boat, *and* we made money on it. The store itself was busy in the morning and wasn't busy again until night.

We'd have a stem of bananas on the boat. They would come in a special banana basket packed with straw or hay. And you could get tarantulas. We got one of them on the supply boat, and it pretty near got away on us. If it had got down under the floorboards of the boat, we'd have been in real trouble. Neil Blewett . . . we had a big, long butcher knife for cutting the bananas off the stalk . . . he made a slash at it and missed it. But we did step on it before it got away.

The next year we traded that boat and got a big boat. It could carry eight tons. When we got this boat, it left every morning at eight o'clock and no fooling about it . . . didn't leave at five after, it pulled out at eight o'clock. That was our main business, much more than the store.

Jack Brown,
Young's Point, Ontario

DOING MICA

*B*efore I was married, I "did mica" for my father. Mica was pieces of rock that went into electrical appliances for insulation. My father went out and got it off the rocks in big pieces, then it was all graded at different prices. I can remember cutting it on the big knife, even up the edges, make it look good, get it ready for market.

My brothers and sisters and I got 3¢ a pound to cull it; eventually that went up to 10¢. You could do 50 pounds a day, so that would be $5, a lot of money then. Sometimes I did the grading, too, when my father didn't have time.

When it was culled and graded, my father would sell it to a company in Hull. They used to ship it from Hull to different countries.

Irene (Boland) Lagacé,
Old Chelsea, Quebec

BACK TO THE COUNTER

*I*n the spring of 1921, we were going in to Fort Norman to stake oil claims. When we arrived at Fort Smith, we met a Mr. Conibear who was a private storekeeper. Most stores along the Mackenzie route were owned by one of the trading companies like Hudson's Bay or Northern Trading or Lampson Hubbard, but his was a privately owned store at Fort Smith.

Mr. Conibear was awaiting the first steamer of the season to take him out. He had staked his claims during the winter. (Everyone up there, who had a pair of snowshoes, went down to Fort Norman and staked claims that winter.) He had been offered $25 000 for his claims by one of the oil companies, but he had turned down the offer and was going out to get a higher price. Some companies had been making fantastic offers, up to $50 000.

So that made us feel good. We thought we'd do all right.

Conibear got to Toronto and on to New York, and the bottom had dropped out of the market. He lost the $25 000, which he should have taken. As far as I know, he never did sell his claims. I imagine he went back to his store a wiser and sadder man.

And the same thing happened to us. When we got out in the fall, there was no market.

Bill Ogilvie,
Fort Smith, Northwest Territories

IN THE NAME OF THE KING

*W*e had sidelines as well. I was Justice of the Peace for quite a few years. We had several interesting cases that we tried. You see, it would take two JPs to make a magistrate. Don Bradley and I were called in on several cases.

There were a couple of Indians brought up before Bradley and I one morning. One was up for having liquor on the reservation. The other one got into a fight and broke his father's arm. It was Provincial Police here at the time, and Gerry Kline was the policeman. Bradley and I gave them six months each. Tough characters. As Gerry Kline took them out of the courtroom, I said, ''Those fellows will never stay in Nelson for six months.''

So about two months later, I was just opening the store in the morning, when Gerry Kline came in and asked, "Have you seen a couple of Indians on the loose?" I just smiled. "Yes," he said, "I remember what you said."

Gerry was very anxious to get these fellows, particularly the one named Swanson. He didn't like to see him loose. So Gerry teamed up with Constable White, he was an old Mountie. They went down around Sidar watching for them. They'd been out about 48 hours and were hiding in the bush. When it was just getting dark, Gerry looked up and he saw a couple of figures walking down the track. They were the two they were after.

Gerry said to Constable White, "What is the procedure in taking them?"

"You pull your revolver and tell them to put their hands up in the name of the King, three times. Then, if they don't put their hands up, you are permitted to shoot." Then he added, "You let me handle this."

Herman Kavelman, in this New Dundee, Ontario store for 72 years, became a legend. He could pull your teeth, fix your watch or put your boyfriend's photo on your fingernail.

Gerry was very glad to let him.

So, just as the two fellows got opposite to them, Constable White jumped up and he yelled, "Hands up, you Sons of Bitches!"

They took them back to Nelson and Swanson escaped again, and he kidnapped an Indian girl. No, he killed his wife first. Then he kidnapped an Indian girl, and headed down to Oregon where they caught him. It was life imprisonment after that.

Arthur Burch,
Wynndel, British Columbia

IN THE BARBER'S CHAIR

*O*ur store in Redvers, Saskatchewan had a pool hall and barbershop. The boys would come in for groceries on Saturday night and stay until one o'clock. It was 50¢ for a haircut and we cut the hair *off*. After supper on a Saturday night, when the harvest excursion boys were in town, they would line up and take a ticket for their turn. Each would be five minutes in the chair.

Bates was the garage man, a six-foot-two fellow, all muscle, and he weighed 350 pounds. He and I had a lot of fracasses together. His grandfather left him a pair of extractors for pulling teeth. This local man came into the barbershop complaining of a toothache, and of course the dentist only came once a week. So Bates and I grabbed him and put him in the barber chair and held him down kicking. Bates gets the pliers at him and into the corner goes the tooth. We had put a red candy into his mouth, and that tooth was really the red candy.

So he gets up and spits into the coal pail. Then he comes back and yells, "You darned buggers pulled out the wrong tooth!"

Louis Rutherford,
Redvers, Saskatchewan

MY MOTHER, THE VET

*T*he Tousants across the road had a cow which got into clover in early summer and bloated. That happened a lot. If you didn't help a cow like that, it would die in a hurry. The usual cure was to take a knife and stick it below a certain rib, which would let the gas escape.

The talk in the store was that they were about to do this, but my mother said, "First take a bottle of ginger ale out of the cooler and give it that." The men laughed, but they did it. And they didn't have to stick the cow. It got better.

Enid Swerdfeger,
Glen Stewart, Ontario

WE WEREN'T GOING TO MAKE IT

*B*ill was an alcoholic, and he and his father, they used to make home brew. They had a bottler and everything. And they would bottle 12 bottles, and then they'd open the first one and start to drink it. And they would *not* drink it until it was bottled. It was sort of their Liquor Control Board.

Barbara, Bill's wife, she had quite a row to hoe. And she had a lot of children. She started into labour one time, and they ran to the store for me. I had a 1936 Ford pick-up truck and I got them in. And he was pretty drunk, and she was just getting terrible. By the time we got half way to Peterborough, it looked to me that we weren't going to make it. And she was screaming, and he kept saying, "Now Barb, just take it easy. You have this one, and I'll have the next one." Which didn't help any. But the baby was born right on the stretcher when we got to the hospital, not inside the hospital, born right in the truck there.

Ontario

WE'RE OUT OF ASHES

*N*ow Dave Bradshaw had the store there and he was right next door to the community hall, and he took care of the coal stove that used to keep the hall warm at night. They had a meeting, they were rural people and they were taxpayers and they hired the secretary of the municipality to give a talk on taxation. He was a fellow that drank and, every time he made a speech, he'd always be tight. He was a good speaker, knew what he was talking about. And the tighter he was, the better talker he was.

Dave had the stove going and there was some ashes in there. And the speaker was tight and he threw up on the platform. It didn't phase him a bit, he kept right on talking. Dave Bradshaw went to the stove and got some ashes and covered it up. We went on for a little while and he threw up again. Dave Bradshaw went back to the stove and he got some more ashes.

But the third time he threw up, Dave Bradshaw says, "Mister Chairman, I move we adjourn the meeting because we've run out of ashes."

Jack Hallett,
Federal, Alberta

184

CHAPTER FOURTEEN

FIRE, FLOOD AND VARIOUS ADVENTURES

Imagine a building built of wood and filled with the comings and goings of humanity, with men smoking pipes and cigarettes and cigars. Picture a big stove kept red hot in an attempt to heat the store building, which was built like a barn. Scatter around drums of coal oil and turpentine. Put some gasoline pumps outside. Pile wood in the shed or heap coal in the basement. It is easy to see that a country store might catch fire. A great many of them did.

If your place of business was by a river on an ocean, damages from flash floods or tidal bores were a possibility. Cyclones or tornados could strike your town. Snowstorms could isolate your village.

Few veteran storekeepers got through their 20 or 30 years of business without one untoward adventure. If you were a Maritime merchant, your ships were at the mercy of the sea. On the prairies, you shared the farmers' dust storms, hailstorms and grasshopper plagues. In northern areas, you had to move your goods across frozen tundra or along icy waters, subject always to the relentless laws of life and death in the North.

And, as if fire, floods and tornados, shipwrecks and scurvy were not enough, there were ghosts!

REBUILDING IT TOGETHER

We lost our first Vernon River store. We didn't have gasoline tanks, just a little building close to the store where we kept barrels of gasoline. A young fellow came at night and wanted gas. My husband and I were getting ready to go to a concert at the Catholic Hall and were just ready to close the store.

My husband said, "I'll just use a flashlight because of the fumes." But this young fellow went into the building and must have had a cigarette. There was an explosion right away. It spread so quickly . . . we had bought turpentine and left it on the steps of the store . . . and the flames spread so quickly.

Father McGuigan stopped the concert and sent everybody down to help. There was very little they could do. We had one little pump and the fire was so fast. We had a lot of flammable stuff in the basement. The irony of it all was that we had coal for the winter stored in the cellar and that was burning for days and days.

But they saved the house, took all the furniture out, in case it would go. The only thing saved from the store was the cash till. Pat Cairns came running down and grabbed that. And he carried the books up to his house. We lost everything else, even the pot-bellied stove in the middle of the store . . . had to buy another stove.

It burned on the 19th of November, and on the 19th of December we moved into our present store for the Christmas trade. First, it snowed for days after the fire and put the coal fire out, and the foundation was still good. Then the people came to help. They said, "We want you in the community, you are just what we needed all these years. You can find the markets for what we grow." (My husband was a good trader and a great organizer.)

"We want you to stay!" Some people come with a load of lumber and boards. Others gave days of work. One man, I remember, came with two bundles of shingles. There would be 15 or 20 men working, as many as could get on the roof at one time. Some of the shingles they put on in 1925 are still there.

We fed them all. My husband's mother was living and she was a very good cook. At night, we would make an awful lot of pies. Three meals right here. We had a priest, Father McGuigan, who was a great organizer. He would stand there and tell the men what to do; most were his own parishioners. We ourselves were Protestant.

Then some fellows came in the evenings to help us paint the boards for the shelves; and then to help us stock the shelves. Just a month from the time it burned, we were in our new store.

Katie MacLeod,
Vernon River, Prince Edward Island

TIDAL BORE

This store at Port au Port, Newfoundland was moved to higher ground after a tidal bore slammed ice floes into the original building and wrecked it in 1951.

We are the oldest firm on the west coast of Newfoundland. My grandfather came here from St. John's, dealt in salt fish, had everything from a needle to an anchor. Grandfather and Father would buy in England, one trip in the spring of the year. Father almost came back on the *Titanic*'s last trip. Something stopped him. I can't remember the exact story, but he was supposed to be on it, and he wasn't.

The store was on the beach over there until a storm wrecked it in December 1951. It was a tidal bore, came in and filled the beach and pushed the ice right through the store. The store had been there since 1886 and never damaged before. It was really a freak thing.

Our car was stuck over there in the flood and we lost it. It was a new Pontiac. When my father was leaving the store that evening, he said, "I can't get that car door open." My cousin tried to get it open, too. "Oh," Father said, "We'll leave it there for tonight." And the next morning, it was ruined along with the store.

It took us two years to build this store on higher ground. We stayed on the beach, in the patched-up old store, while we had this one built.

Patricia Abbott,
Port au Port, Newfoundland

BRIDGE OUT

We had considerable flooding every spring, as there were three creeks within a mile of the store. The trouble with crossing a flooded bridge was that often the bridge itself didn't hold. BRIDGE OUT was the sign that often appeared on country roads in the spring.

One time, Mildred was with a carload of ladies going to a WCTU (Women's Christian Temperance Union) meeting. Mabel, a very sedate lady in other respects, was a wild car driver. They were travelling very fast along a gravel road and were suddenly poised on the incline of a bridge over the creek, when one of the ladies read the sign and screamed, "Bridge out!"

Fortunately, the bridge had been put back in, but at the speed Mabel was driving, Mildred said afterwards, that it might not have mattered.

Milton Swerdfeger,
Glen Stewart, Ontario

BLOWN AWAY

The merchant vessels going to St. John's in the fall, shipping fish and picking up cargo, would run into storms. There was no radar in the early days. And it was all sail, too.

Maybe you've heard of Captain Joby Barber. He was 48 days adrift. He left St. John's with a load of general cargo for Newtown and he blew across the Atlantic in a storm.

He left along with many other vessels, and they all got drifted off. Most of the vessels got back. The crew of one, I believe, was picked off by a steamer. But Barber lost his spars and his sails. They got back so far, close enough to see Newfoundland, but then another storm came up. It drove him across for 48 days and he got into Tobermory, Scotland.

He had any amount of food; he'd been putting home with a load of provisions for the winter. But they got very low on water because it should have been a 12-hour trip home to Bonavista Bay.

This happened back in the 1930s. He's alive now, 80-odd years. Comes from a wonderful family. He's a very dear friend of ours.

My cousin, who was master of his own vessel, was there in St. John's that day. He was bringing a load for all the merchants of Twillingate and Herring Neck and the areas around. But he wouldn't leave. He was only young, but he knew his barometer . . . if any man ever knew his barometer, he did. He learned that from his father. His brothers kept on at him, because the rest of the vessels were sailing out.

He went up through the watch-house and Bowrings' Premises to the theatre in the afternoon . . . something he had never done before . . . just to get away from his brothers and the crew. When he came back from the theatre through the watch-house, he was covered with snow. The watchman said, "What? Is it dirty, Skipper?"

He said, "Yes, it's a bad day. Gonna be a bad night." This was late in the fall, it got dark around half-past three or four o'clock.

"My gosh, my son is on one of those vessels."

Earlier, when my cousin had heard the other ships were going, he had said, "Well, they'll be back."

Well, they did come back, some of them. Others didn't get back so easily. And Barber drifted across the Atlantic. But no loss of life! Barber's mother never gave up hope for him. She kept praying for him every night. For 48 days.

Bill Ashbourne and Herb Gillett,
Twillingate, Newfoundland

GOD'S WILL

*T*he storekeeper was a Ukrainian immigrant, short and slow-moving, a soft-spoken scholar and a deeply religious man. He often read when there were no customers around, and he loved to share the news of a Bible passage with a customer. His wife was short and chatty and, in moments of stress, had the habit of shredding paper into tiny bits with her fingers. One day, she absent-mindedly shredded a farmer's grain cheque that he had handed her. She was sometimes impatient when her husband did not get around to fixing something, or when he tried to calm troubled waters by saying, "It is God's will."

"Ah!" she would sigh. "It is indeed strange how often your will and God's are the same!"

One night, fire destroyed their store and living quarters, and the family escaped with nothing but the clothes on their backs. "It is God's will!" said the storekeeper sadly, as he gathered his wife and six children around him. "So we must accept it. And are we not truly blessed that no one was injured!"

"Indeed," said his wife. "But it might have helped if you had cleaned the chimney like I asked you to."

Walter Dziadow,
Valley River, Manitoba

CHINOOKS AND A CYCLONE

We've lived here 60 years. Lots of snow, but we get Chinook winds too. Any time of year. A west wind comes over the mountains and it's a warm wind. You see a Chinook arch and in a short time you get the balmiest breezes.

The first year we were here, my brother and mother came up for Christmas, and we got a buggy to go out to our homestead to show them how many logs Joe had put on the house and everything. We had a buggy and team and we had to go across the river, and coming back I was scared to death. The Chinook was so strong that the water on the river came right up to the hub of the wheel on the buggy. It had melted that fast.

The cyclone was in July 1927. We were lucky. We didn't have any damage to our store. It blew a lot of shops down on Main Street. Took one hardware store right off, landed it on the other side of the street. We were away on holidays. The fellow we had in the store said that the roof just lifted right up and sat right down again. And afterwards we never had any leakage at all.

We were coming home across the border and we had a sticker on our car from Rocky Mountain House. The man said, "Oh, there's been a cyclone at Rocky Mountain House." And I said, "Never!"

No one got badly hurt. One fellow got hit by a board. One couple had their house, everything, taken right away and all their silver was scattered all over town. People were picking up silver of theirs all over.

Then it went right up the main street, took out the hardware store and almost took the bank. This fellow who had the hardware store, his home was behind the Imperial Bank and he had a garage at the back of it. It hit his store, and then he wanted to go home to see how his wife was, and he went to put his car in the garage, and the garage was whipped right away from him. So he thought the Lord was really treating him poorly.

That gust of wind went up and hit the school, took all the trees all down. There were steps up to the school and it wedged pieces of trees right into the wood of the steps.

Joe and Jenny Cony,
Rocky Mountain House, Alberta

AFTER THE FIRE

We lost everything in the fire, our books, all our stock. We had our new things in for Christmas, stacked up everywhere, lines up to hang things on, a shipment of china just unpacked.

The night watchman at the lumber mill saw the fire, but instead of coming and telling us, he took time to put a fire in the furnace and get enough steam to blow the whistle. By that time, the store was too far gone.

We called the fire department in Florenceville and they saved the house. It would have gone. The fire was so hot that afterwards you could see where the oil melted out of the paint and ran down in big drops, then dried when the cold water struck it. We had thin nylon curtains on the living room and I was afraid they'd catch, so I just jerked them right off. We had a stand of paint in the store window. When that got hot, those cans of paint were coming across the road like something out of a gun. Our stove-oil drum exploded; it was on the veranda of the store and it blew.

We did get a few things out of the basement afterward. Next day, the men from the mill came with a big forklift and lifted our small safe out, and brought it over here to the shed. We couldn't open it for three weeks. If you open a safe that has been through the fire, as soon as you can handle the dials, the minute you open the door, everything inside will burn.

We got out a crate of oranges. They were as good as ever, but black; you couldn't wash the black off. We had a brand new refrigerator, and meat had just come in from Canada Packers. The ham was delicious afterward, only the paper burned off the outside of it. That refrigerator just parted company, the sides went their way, the door fell out one way and the back the other way. But the meat was beautiful.

We owned the piece of land across the street by the house, but the Liberal government had not allowed us to build on it. My father-in-law had been a Conservative member of the legislature for 15 years. But by now the government was Conservative again. The store burned on Thursday morning, and on Friday, December 11, we went to Fredericton for a permit to build. Hugh John Fleming called in the Provincial Planning Officer and told him to have a letter in the mail next morning. He said, "You go ahead anyway, even if you don't get it." And he told the Planning Officer to be up at Stickney on Monday morning.

So the very next morning, the bulldozer from the mill started digging. On the day after Christmas, early in the morning, we poured the foundation for the store when it was 30° below (Fahrenheit). We had a man who worked for the government and had equipment for heating water, and he kept the water boiling. It was finished at 12 o'clock that night. We opened for business on the 6th of March. Some of our customers paid their store bill by working on the new store.

When we lost all our books and bills in the fire, I sat down that very morning and listed all the people who owed us and the amounts I thought they owed. About 15 came and paid. One man said, "I have my slips for all but last week's groceries and each week is about $11, so just put $11 down for last week, too." But there were about 60 that didn't pay.

Mae Melville,
Stickney, New Brunswick

THE MILL FIRE

We almost lost the store again when the mill burned, because there was a terrific wind and the stuff was dropping all around the store. Stanley was away to Woodstock.

About 11 o'clock in the morning, one of the men, who drove a truck from the mill, came in and wanted ice cream. I put the cover up on the freezer and couldn't see much. "What in the world is making it so dark?" We had a small window there that looked out toward the mill. I looked out and these great black clouds of smoke were coming.

He said, "Mill's on fire!" He jumped in the truck, backed into the end of the mill and began hooking off the wagons of lumber. (These were wagons they would fill with different sizes of lumber as they came through the mill.) As long as they could, the men hauled these away . . . .

I phoned to Woodstock to tell Stanley he had better come home. He was only 17 minutes getting to our road, but the last half mile took longer because he was caught in such a crowd of cars.

At the side of the store was all grass and weeds, and I had to keep running around to see it wasn't catching in the grass. A couple of men came and watched the outside of the store. We had a pile of wood at the back and there was an old jute bag fallen down between the wood and the store. Sparks from the mill dropped on that, but the men caught it before it got going.

We always had a fear of fire. And the insurance companies weren't too happy about giving us insurance because we were so handy to the mill.

Mae Melville,
Stickney, New Brunswick

IN MY HOMBURG HAT

*A*fter a particularly difficult experience when a friend's house burned down, we decided in our community to purchase a small, used siren from War Assets Corporation, so that people could be warned whenever we had a fire. For years this served the purpose from where it was placed on the roof of the hardware store. Whenever the siren blew, all the business people grabbed their fire extinguishers and ran to the hardware store.

On one occasion, one of the local grain-buyers' houses was on fire. Smoke was pouring out of the roof, windows and doors, and the family was not at home. Really, none of us knew that much about fighting a fire and, at first, we had difficulty in locating the blaze.

We crawled in the back door on our hands and knees, across the kitchen floor, then rushed out again to breathe. Eventually, we decided that the blaze was near the chimney in the basement and we broke the windows and, using our fire extinguishers, we finally controlled the blaze. Afterward, we

194

When silver and gold attracted men to the Northern Ontario bush, stores sprang up overnight, but many disappeared again in raging forest fires which wiped out whole towns. This store is at Porquis Junction near Timmins.

found that the floor joists under the kitchen were nearly burned through, and we were very fortunate that the floor had not given way as we crawled across it. The smoke was so heavy that for two days afterward I coughed constantly.

Over the years, we saved a number of buildings despite our ignorance. Our home was on the upper floor of our store, which was the typical box-frame building with a separate staircase to the upper level. One early morning, as we slept, we were awakened by the local school teacher, "Don, Don, the ice house is on fire!" I looked out the window and I nearly fainted. This large frame building was burning furiously just behind our next-door neighbour's hotel; and my building was about three feet from the hotel.

I pulled on a pair of pants, grabbed two pails of water. I had a new green Homburg hat which I valued greatly, as it was my first purchase of civilian clothing after the war. For some reason I put that on my head and, in my bare feet, I raced down to the rear of the hotel. By wetting down the rear of the hotel, we kept it from burning; also, the wind was blowing straight away from it and that helped. However, the heat and the flames were beginning to threaten the shack of an old fellow named Bill Miller, which stood about 50 feet away. I thought, "Holy Moses, this fire's going to burn old Bill's house down."

So I grabbed two pails of water. And I had on my Homburg hat, my pyjamas top, and my pants were loose, and no shoes on my feet. And I went roaring over with these two pails of water and, as I threw the one, my hat fell off. And I threw the next pail and filled my Homburg hat full of water. You do funny things when you're excited.

Don Wilkes,
Benalto, Alberta

GETTING MARRIED IN GOLDFIELDS

*A*fter surveying the area, I was told to go to Fort Chipewyan at the west end of Lake Athabasca and load up with supplies for the new post, and take them down the 135 miles to Goldfields, and there negotiate for a building and land for the new store.

At Fort Chipewyan, I was given a fair-sized, motor-driven scow loaded to the gunnels with merchandise, plus a few passengers. After an overnight voyage, we came into the lovely little bay where the town or settlement of Goldfields was located. At the entrance to the bay was the Consolidated Mining & Smelting Gold Mine with head frame up and mill buildings taking shape.

I found a few log buildings already in place . . . one a hotel and another a store, plus some shacks. A Mr. Jack Cairns had a small log building on his lot, which was very central. I got it and the lot for $400, moved the goods into it, set up a big tent for a warehouse and, on the back of the lot up against a rock, a tent for Joe Sinclair and I to live in. We were doing business very quickly.

That fall a quantity of fir lumber arrived, plus windows etc., and a nice-sized store was soon ready. I moved in with Howard Souch, the JP and Mining Recorder, and in February of 1936 asked my wife-to-be to come to Goldfields for the marriage as I was not able to get away.

The only snag to the marriage was that there was no one who could perform the ceremony as there was no minister. My fiancée went to the Saskatchewan Government, and the only solution was to the effect that they could pass an order-in-council authorizing Howard Souch to act if he consented.

He declined.

So I told him I would radio out his refusal to the government department in Regina, but I did not tell him that the message was mistyped and was in the affirmative. And so I was able to get married as a result.

Ralph Butchart,
Goldfields, Saskatchewan

HAVING A BABY UP THERE

*T*he first of our two children was due in December, so my wife, Billi, decided to fly out to her sister in Regina as there was no hospital in Goldfields. The air trip out was to be to Prince Albert, maybe 300 miles away, then by train to Regina.

Flying conditions in November, before the big lake froze, were hazardous because of fog. Bill Windrum was flying this route. One November morning with a low ceiling, Billi left. Fifty or 100 miles out, Windrum was forced down due to icing and low ceiling. Billi started to have labour pains and they had to spend the night in the bush.

Next morning, conditions were very poor for flying, but the baby was getting close to being born, so Windrum took off, flew at tree-top for a while, saw a river he recognized, followed it and got into Isle à la Crosse. Half an hour after landing, our first child, a girl, Jacqueline, was born in the hospital there.

Ralph Butchart,
Goldfields, Saskatchewan

GHOSTS

*W*e've got a ghost in this store. I don't care what anybody says, I've heard it twice. Once we were sitting here in this back room; Sheila was sitting there and we were playing Crib and I heard these footprints upstairs and there was nobody living upstairs at the time. I looked up and I said, "Sheila, did you hear that?"

She's looking at her cards and she says, "Yes, I did, and I'm not looking up."

There's one room upstairs over in the corner, where we always hear the noise. Ed was in the office one night about one o'clock in the morning doing a night deposit and he heard something. He went upstairs and looked, couldn't see anything, so he came back down. And he heard it again. He said the hairs just stood up on his back. So he went home.

One couple living upstairs had their dining-room suite in the middle of the floor. They got up one morning and the whole thing was pushed toward the bannister. "Whether I walked in my sleep . . . " Al says, "I don't know, but that thing was not there when I went to bed at night."

Brenda lived upstairs for a while. After she had moved out, she came in and said, "You never told me there was a ghost upstairs."

"Well, I don't like to scare people off. Did anything happen to you?"

"One thing that was really strange. Over by the kitchen, I could have sworn I heard somebody walking upstairs."

I sort of smiled and I said, "You know, Brenda, at one time there were stairs up the side of the building."

We have a friend who is psychic. Bob came driving by here one night, and afterward he said to me, "Do you ever have nice wallpaper up in that bedroom in the corner!"

I said, "There is no wallpaper up there."

He says, "Come on! I was driving by here the other night, and there was a little guy looking out the window and I saw this beautiful blue wallpaper."

"No way, Bob."

"Really and truly. I looked up there, and there was a little guy sitting in the window looking north and the light was on and the wallpaper really struck me."

One of the storekeepers who passed away here (the one who took the heart attack), that's who he described.

Val Holm,
Heffley Creek, British Columbia

CHAPTER FIFTEEN

TROUBLE AND TRAGEDY

Mostly life was good at the corner store. But, when something terrible happened, it happened to everyone in the community, because you were all one big family. The boy who drowned used to ride his bike to the store and play with your kids. Or the man who was killed when his tractor overturned, was a favourite customer. For many nights afterward, the conversation in the store was grim. Maybe a chair or a nail keg was noticeably empty.

The fires were the worst. You knew those three little girls who didn't escape, and their small faces haunt you yet.

But life had to go on. Whether it was the customer's family or the storekeeper's family struck by tragedy, you all got together and buried the bodies, built up the house or store again, closed the ranks of your community family. And carried on.

THE TRAGEDY OF THE BRIDES

John Joseph Walsh had two daughters who were to be married on the same day, and everything was ready for the wedding. A brother and sister who were away had come home. On the day before the wedding, the young people stopped at our store and got a lot of things for tomorrow, and then they were gone into Charlottetown for some more. The brother was driving.

So it was getting very late and we knew they should have been back and we began to worry. We even got out our car and started down the road to look for them, but the fog was so bad we had to turn around.

What happened was right in Charlottetown. The brother who was driving thought he was on the wrong road . . . in the fog he couldn't see a thing . . . and he tried to turn around. While turning, he drove right off the Charlottetown wharf. Both the girls who were to be married drowned, and the brother who was driving drowned. Two of the others, a brother and a sister were saved. The girl's coat caught on a nail on the wharf and that saved her. It was 1928 or 1929, and I think it was an open car that went in.

It was awful. The tables were all set up out on the lawn under the trees, but the wedding became a funeral. The brides were laid out in their white wedding dresses.

The parents never got over it. Afterward, the mother never wanted to talk about it. It would have been better for the father if he could have talked it out. But she wouldn't let him talk about it.

One of the young grooms later married the sister, the girl that was saved by her coat catching on a nail.

Katie MacLeod,
Vernon River, Prince Edward Island

PHILIP

This little Philip was an orphan from a Home, staying with a local family named Snelgrove. An old diary tells about him. He started school, and he was coming down the hill there on a toboggan and he hit a stone at our corner and was seriously hurt internally. So they brought him into this store and put him into the bedroom off the store.

When the lady of the store was upstairs doing her housework, Philip got out of bed and began to bleed more internally.
So it was a matter of life and death for weeks and weeks. This
old diary tells who sat up with Philip each night.

Before the accident, Mrs. Annie Snelgrove had died and
Philip had stayed on with her grown-up son. But the Home
wouldn't allow an orphan to stay in a home where there was no
woman to look after him. So, by the time he got better, they
told him he had to go back to the Home and this is when he
cried and cried and cried that he had to leave Camborne.

Doris Emond,
Camborne, Ontario

THEY BURNT HIM OUT

*I*rvine Junkin had a general store in Bobcaygeon in the 1880s.
He ran the post office, too, and was Justice of the Peace.
Because of his activities in the temperance movement, they
burnt him out.

The hotel people wanted the liquor. Local men would go
and work all winter in the lumber camps and, of course, there
were people here in Bobcaygeon just ready to take their money.
First stop was the bars, and there they played poker. We had
one fellow here they called John D. Rockefeller. He used to
play poker with them as soon as they got out, and what the
bars didn't take he did. They used to let the liquor flow pretty
freely and get the fellows pretty tight, and then they didn't play
cards so well.

The temperance movement became strong because of the
violence that went with the drinking, and because their wives
and children were neglected. The men would cash their
cheques in the early spring and were broke when it came time
to bring the logs down through the rivers. The same gang was
waiting for their money when they got out again.

Between Bobcaygeon and Kinmount it's 17 or 18 miles and
there were 17 taverns. The lumbermen would go into these and
get drinking, and then they'd go out and fight. They'd tackle
each other with axes, take right after each other with the axes
they had to work with.

Irvine Junkin was one of the leaders in the temperance
movement. I guess there was a little financial motive involved

because the lumbermen didn't pay their store bills. He would carry the wives and family all winter and, instead of him getting paid, it all went to the drink.

It would be the hotelkeepers and their customers who burned the store. You see the temperance people were trying to close the bars. Bobcaygeon was split about 50-50. A lot of the women were temperance workers and the men were the drinkers. The Bobcaygeon fire engine was a little engine with a pumper, and they had to light it up and get the steam up. But the night they burned the Junkin store, they had let the water all out of the tanks. So, it was planned. The firefighters didn't get the water there and the steam up until the place was burned down.

The temperance movement did close the bars. It was a dry town for a long, long time.

Dr. Doug Thomas,
Bobcaygeon, Ontario

THE 1918 FLU

*I*n 1905, Klaas Reimer built a new store. He died the year after the store was built, and then his sons continued. Two sons were involved at first, then only one, and he did very, very well. His name was Jacob W. Reimer, the one who died of the flu in 1918.

I remember the flu epidemic very well. I had the flu, too. One night I didn't feel like undressing, just got upstairs to my bedroom and curled around the stove-pipe and slept on the floor there. After that I was on my feet again. When I was over this bout, I walked to Steinbach to help in the improvised school-hosptial and I found it difficult to walk the mile and a half. There was one trained nurse at the hospital, and she was not fully trained.

Jacob died at home. I think they had to close the store at times while the flu was on. There were only four men at his funeral, and they had to bury him as well. The others were all down in bed. The men who had made his coffin and put him in it, they took him past the house, so his own sick family could see him through the window.

John C. Reimer,
Steinbach, Manitoba

BURNING THE COMPANY STORES

In Glace Bay, you either fished or you worked in the mines. The storekeeper supplied the fishermen with boots and rope and hooks, and sometimes even with his boat. By the time the fisherman put out to sea, he owed his soul to the merchant. Then the merchant decided the price of fish and always made sure the fisherman was left owing him a little.

When a fisherman's kid or a miner's kid went to the store to get groceries, the merchant would always say, "Did your mother send you?" He'd be buying on credit. If a kid was lucky, he might manage to sneak a chocolate into the order.

Until 1925, all the stores around Glace Bay were company stores owned by the mining companies. That year, the miners went on strike and were locked out of the company stores. Their families were hungry and they were desperate. So they burned the stores to the ground. The company never tried to establish company stores again.

Bill McNeil,
Glace Bay, Nova Scotia

John C. Reimer stands beside a replica of the Reimer store in the Mennonite Village Museum at Steinbach, Manitoba. His uncle, Jacob W. Reimer, was a young, ambitious storekeeper in 1918 when the Spanish flu epidemic killed him and thousands of others across Canada.

LIGHTNING STRIKES TWICE

Sometimes Grandfather would rent the store out, while he gave his attention to the farm. It was rented to Gilmour at the time it was hit by lightning. I was sitting in the east window of the house and saw it hit some cattle in the field. Two of them died. I didn't know until later about the tragedy at the store.

At that time the Orange Lodge met upstairs above the store. On the evening of the storm, my father was there attending an Orange Lodge meeting, with most of the men of the neighbourhood. He saw what happened.

A steel support rod ran across the ceiling under the rafters of the big building. The lightning came down the chimney and followed the steel rod in both directions. Among the crowd of men were a father and son sitting on opposite sides of the room. The bolt of lightning singled each of them out and killed them both.

Bernard Redner,
Rednersville, Ontario

MOTHER'S SKUNK

Everybody was in our Cape Negro store waiting for the mail, when the dog chased a skunk underneath the store. There was a stone foundation around the store and there was a window with a shutter. We would take the shutter out so the wind would blow under and make it cooler. And this shutter was open. When the dog chased the skunk, it just jumped in there. We think the skunk was alive in there for two or three days and finally died in there. We didn't realize that at the time, thought it had gone.

It nearly bankrupted my mother, because the odour went into everything. Everything ruined, other than the canned goods. She had flour in the store, oatmeal, everything in bulk . . . we had to feed all that stuff to our hens.

My poor mother, I don't know how she lived through that. She had worked so hard for that store and the post office. My sea-captain father was home sick at the time; he'd been hurt on his ship; a boom or something had hit him. She had five kids to look after and three cows to milk. We kids fetched and carried, but what could anyone do?

It broke her heart really. It was such a disaster. Even on the yards of cotton, you could smell it. She did all kinds of things trying to get the odours out. She tried washing things off with vinegar. She even rendered down the lard, but it didn't help.

But she survived. Some of the wholesalers gave her credit, and she restocked the store. My father didn't want her to, he was sick and it was just too overpowering. It was six or eight months before she got the building back to normal and built up her trade again.

Joseph Ross,
Cape Negro, Nova Scotia

MURDERED

*N*else and Lily Tousant had the small farm across from the Glen Stewart store. Nelse was a character right out of Dickens, bent and twisted, but with a twinkle in his eye, gregarious and fun-loving, ignorant in the sense of being uneducated, but not all that ignorant in the ways of the world. The two small girls who lived at the store loved his barns, his horse and wagon which we could help drive, his cows which we were allowed to fetch for milking, even his geese which chased us.

His wife, Lily, was an excellent cook who made delicious homemade buns and grew luscious strawberries in her garden every June. She was also a hypochondriac, always afraid she was about to die. She used to wake up at night to see if her heart was beating. In addition, she worried about violence and crime of every sort. She kept Mother listening for hours to her troubles. Mother, leaning on the candy counter, reassured her as best she could, while longing to get back to her own housework.

Nelse died of cancer in 1955 in his 80s. Lily was twenty years younger and lived on alone long after. Even today, I hate to recall how she died in the early 1970s. Worried and anxious all her life, but too fiercely independent to leave her home at the last, she took care of herself and hid her money under the bed.

On a summer night in 1975, her house burned. The store, which had always given her support and protection, was vacant at the time, caught between one of the several ownership changes which have occurred since 1959. In the ruins of her house, it was found that Lily Tousant died tied to a chair, murdered for the small amount of cash she kept under the bed. Her murderers have never been found.

Enid Swerdfeger,
Glen Stewart, Ontario

AS IF IT HAD COME TO LIFE

*I*n the early part of my first winter at Goldfields, an elderly trapper, 50 miles west of us, shot his young partner at point blank range, through the mouth. The RCMP persuaded him to surrender when he holed up in his cabin, and they brought him in for preliminary hearing to Goldfields. My friend, Howard Souch, was the JP for the hearing.

The body of the murdered man had frozen solid, in a rather grotesque position. I recall his right arm was bent with fingers near his mouth, as though in dying he had tried to reach the bullet at the back of his head. In order for the body to fit into a coffin, it first had to be thawed out. The only building for this purpose was the log building I had bought and which was now a warehouse.

The RCMP were able to elevate the murdered man on a platform close to a roaring wood heater. It took a long time, and a policeman was always on duty. Late one night, I called in to chat with the constable and, while conversing, the body must have thawed enough in places to upset its balance, and it tumbled with quite a crash onto the floor. It was as if it had come to life, and it was a very scary experience.

The next year, the Bank of Montreal decided to open a branch. Again the same problem . . . no building for them to operate out of until their own was built. The warehouse stocks were low, so I offered them the log building. It was a little cramped for them but they managed. It was not too long, however, before they complained about the place having a peculiar odour. Knowing it was the result of thawing out a corpse, I thought it better to say it came from storage of beaver and muskrat pelts.

Ralph Butchart,
Goldfields, Saskatchewan

This store at Nipissing near North Bay, Ontario would have to deal with the good times and the bad times of its customers . . . prospectors, loggers and adventurers in the Northern Ontario bush.

THE BURNING

*J*ost was a teacher in the separate school just outside of town. He was an intelligent, educated man, but a strange and lonely man. He married a lady who already had a family, then they had additional family. They lived on a farm just outside town. Things were not working out too well with the two families.

He went out to the barn where there were cattle and horses, and made winnows of straw and set them on fire. Then he went into the house and got all the children with him (they were all his children; she was away with the ones that were hers alone). He set the fire then in the house.

He sat on the oldest daughter to keep her from escaping. But then the smaller children, crying and screaming, took his attention, and when he went to them, she got away and got out the window. It was wintertime and she ran almost a mile in her nightgown, to another house.

Then we got out there. But the whole house was burned down. The doctor was there and a group from town that acted sort of like an inquest. They were mostly veterans. Vera's dad was a veteran. He had been in the Boer War, lied about his age at sixteen. Then he came to Canada and worked in Ferrier's Store, then joined the First World War, and came back to run the Co-op store. So he was out there, and they were sifting through the ashes, looking for the bones. But the reaction of the veterans was the worst. The smell of burnt flesh created too many memories, so they were worse than the civilians.

Then they were bringing up the bones from the basement which the house had collapsed into. They had to account for each member of the family. I had gone out there with Crawford Gillespie who ran the undertaking establishment. I can remember Jost's body was just a stump, no head, no legs. Coming into town, I sort of held it on the back of this truck.

Maldwyn Hughes,
Lemberg, Saskatchewan

CHAPTER SIXTEEN

WAITING OUT THE WAR

For some people, the war was all too immediate . . . they had two sons in it. For others, it was a time of inconvenience, of rationing, of War Time Price and Trade Board restrictions.

It shaped the pattern of business in stores across Canada. In the 1930s, you had it and couldn't sell it. In the 1940s, you could sell anything you got, but you couldn't get it.

There were a few merchants who set up their black markets, who found ways around the restrictions and rationing. Most dealt with it honestly, doling out the molasses and sugar and tea as fairly as they could.

And always you waited for the war to be over, for the bad news to end, for the good news of victory, for the boys to come back.

They came back . . . or some of them did . . . and sat around the stove again. They told stories of what it was like, and some of them couldn't forget, couldn't adjust to the quiet country life again.

The store itself was like that. The Depression, followed by the World War, had extended the old way of life and kept the position of the country store intact. But after the war, the old patterns could no longer hold. The country store would have to forge ahead and adopt new ways, become progressive in the 1950s, and compete with the supermarkets in the city. Change would be the order of the day.

ALL THE HEARTBREAK AND JOY

*W*hat I can remember about the store was that it was a 24-hour-a-day service, and people around the district spent all their spare time in there. Especially in the evening. It was very lively in the evenings. People would come in just after supper to get their groceries, and then they'd stay because other people would be in there doing the same thing. They'd be talking and laughing and telling jokes.

There'd be old war stories about the First World War. Later on, we went right through the Second World War. All the people would be talking about getting letters from their sons in the armed services, all the news about them, where they were and how they were. All the heartbreak and joy mixed in with the world situation at that time. And it was all there in the general store . . . talked about.

There were four trains a day that put mail off, two trains each way. So people were coming in for their mail, and mailing letters and money orders to the catalogue places.

Country stores waited quietly with many benches and barrels and chairs empty during the war. In every community there were young men who never came back.

It was the centre where people talked everything over, everything that came up. And sometimes it was *sad*, the news that they'd get. Somebody would be there that would care, that would want to hear about it or be with them. Especially during the war, I remember that happening. Or somebody would be missing and they would worry and worry and wonder when they'd hear in the mail . . . .

Corine (McGarry) Stillborn,
Finnie, Saskatchewan

SOMETHING TERRIBLE IN HALIFAX

*T*he Halifax Explosion was in 1917, when the ship *Mont Blanc*, full of ammunition, blew up. People all around here knew something terrible had happened at nine o'clock in the morning, because all the dishes rattled in all the houses. They thought the Germans had landed.

The telephone's Central was in Barrington and she would get the news. But it was all day before we found out what had happened. The first news was that the Germans had blown up a ship in Halifax Harbour and Halifax was completely destroyed. Various other reports came in later, but it was a day or so before they really knew what had happened.

A special train came through from Boston with doctors, nurses, and medical supplies, linens, bandages, everything.

Joseph Ross,
Cape Negro, Nova Scotia

4¢ WORTH

*I*n the '40s when the war was on, you could sell anything you had. People didn't have gas to go to town. It was a seller's market then, if you could get the goods.

But we had this War Time Prices and Trade Board. Those inspectors were a bunch of devils. They would descend on you very suddenly. They would go through your place with a fine tooth comb, and, of course, you'd be terrified in case you had overcharged for something or other, so that you'd have to appear before the board.

All the ration coupons, too! I remember this one family came every day for 5¢-worth of sugar when sugar was 8¢ a pound. By the time you weighed that up and had to use your bag and your string . . . ! And this was every day! So when these coupons came out rationing sugar, my husband said, "Well, thank God, that will stop her from buying 5¢-worth of sugar."

But there were also these fruit, jam and jelly coupons, and two of them were the equivalent of a coupon for one pound of sugar. So then they came and asked for a half pound of sugar . . . one fruit coupon. So now we were down to 4¢!

Jean (Weir) Drimmie,
Lang, Ontario

FIVE GALLONS OF WATER

*W*e had inspectors from the War Time Prices and Trade Board. They'd come round. They would check your charge accounts, your sales slips. Or if you were reported, they'd come in and go through everything in the store. The public were told to keep a record, and if any storekeeper charged them too much, they should report it.

They were fair. I know one time I was reported for a can of salmon. I sold it at that time for 25¢. You were told by the War Time Prices and Trade Board what mark-up you could take. And this was right at Christmas and the girls were busy. On the shelf above the salmon, I had grapefruit juice and that was 27¢. And the girl made a mistake, she wrote down 27¢ for the salmon. I was reported for that.

The inspector came out and he worked from 9:30 in the morning 'til nine o'clock at night, checked all my invoices, my charge accounts and everything else. And he said he couldn't understand anybody reporting me. So I didn't get fined. It was an error.

It was a customer reported me, but he was head of another store. A good, strong Co-op man, put it that way.

The only inspectors I would say weren't fair were the gas spotters. They were pretty dirty. They would sit across the street and watch to see if you gave anybody gas after seven o'clock. You couldn't give it after seven at night and you couldn't give it before seven o'clock in the morning. And you were supposed to tear the coupon out of the book before you put the gas in.

An inspector pulled into one person's place there and wanted gas, and it was after seven. The storekeeper said, "No, its closed."

He said, "Well, haven't you got any inside?"

The storekeeper said, "Hmn, there's a five-gallon can there."

"Put it in."

"No, you can put it in yourself."

So the man got the five-gallon can and put it in himself. Of course, then he handed the storekeeper a summons. And he set off going to Regina and he just got nicely out on the road when his car stopped. He had put five gallons of water in. And it was 20 degrees below zero.

Then he came back and wanted this fellow to pull him into town and he wouldn't do it. He hadn't put the water in, just said there's a can over there. So the inspector couldn't do a thing about it.

Herbie Stillborn,
Duff, Saskatchewan

SUGAR IN A CLOVERSEED BAG

*L*ots of times during the war years, you could pick up things in the country stores that you couldn't buy in the bigger centres, because they were rationed. Like butter . . . farmers would bring butter into the store and there were no coupons for farmers' butter. But sugar was rationed; tea and flour were rationed. Gas was rationed.

There was one storekeeper at Argyle who bartered for goods. If you came in with a bag of grain or some chickens, he would trade with you. He took over his father's debts when he started and he died a wealthy man. During the war years, he acquired an old elevator and he stored things you were supposed to have coupons for . . . rationed goods. I don't know how or where he got them.

I bought a hundred of sugar one time in a bag that was labelled "Cloverseed" . . . the sugar bag was inside the cloverseed bag. I got tires at different times . . . which were certainly rationed. He seemed to always have pretty near anything you would ask him for.

During the war, he ordered in several carloads of wire fencing, and he had it around some time and the manufacturers offered to buy it back from him because it had gone up in price so much, but he wouldn't sell it.

By today's standards, his store was anything else but a place to go and buy food. It was a mess. I walked into this store and found the cat lying in the cookie box; I actually did.

You would ask this fellow for a carburetor for instance, and he'd say, "Well, if you're not in a hurry, I think maybe I could find it." And he'd come out with it from under a pile of overalls. People used to drive for miles and miles to get to that store when things were hard to get.

Earl Mark,
Lindsay, Ontario

BLACK MARKET

*W*hen we had rationing during the war, it was "How much can I get?" But the Magdalen Islands were not rationed because they were an outpost and we had special permission from the government to supply them.

There was a black market going on sometimes. I could tell, if a fellow used to buy 10 bags of sugar and now he ordered 20, that he was giving it at a higher price to someone else. We would ship the goods to Souris to go on the boat to the Magdalen Islands. Sometimes the stuff would never leave Souris. They would sell it to somebody right here on Prince Edward Island.

They would get caught sometimes, too. The Mounties would come to me and say, "You know Joe Doe. What did you send him last month? How much did he get this month?" Then he'd be cut off and we couldn't supply him anymore. He would be fined, too, probably $100.

Molasses was sold on the black market a lot. It came in to us by boat and, before rationing, we would probably get 1000 puncheons. Then, in war years we might get 100 and there would be 1000 storekeepers wanting it. So we started breaking it down. The first molasses I ever saw in paper cartons was

packaged at DeBloise Bros. We got a machine and put it in cases of cartons, so we could give it to 10 fellows instead of one.

Gerald Nantes,
Charlottetown, Prince Edward Island

DOLING OUT THE DARK NEWS

Mother was the telegraph operator on the north island near Twillingate. The news came in by telegraph and she would write it out and post it up. And she would get the list of casualties for the town. After the office closed, she would have to go around and deliver the telegrams by foot.

Sometimes the news was so grave and families were so upset that she would hold back the names and give them out gradually. It was just too much.

Mrs. H. Gillett,
Twillingate, Newfoundland

REMEMBRANCE

You know everybody is always running children down. Well, these two little kids came into the store right around Remembrance Day . . . and the Legion always leaves a little container of poppies, so we had this sitting on the counter. Each of these kids had a dime to spend and they were looking at the penny candy and trying to decide. Then they spotted the poppies and they put their dimes . . . both of them . . . into the poppy jar.

That was so beautiful. It just restored my faith.

Val Holm,
Heffley Creek, British Columbia

CHAPTER SEVENTEEN

STOREKEEPERS' KIDS

The storekeeper had his own kids; he also had all the kids in the community. And, one way or another, all the kids in the community had the storekeeper, either as someone they loved or someone they feared, or sometimes as someone they tormented outrageously.

Without exception, adults, who remember being kids, give the candy counter first place in their memory bank. They remember jawbreakers, enormous peppermints, licorice, Long Tom Popcorn, cinnamon stick candy, O-Pee-Chee Bubble Gum, Crackerjack and humbugs. They remember whether the man behind the counter would come and serve you when you tapped your nickel on the glass top, and whether he was cross when you changed your mind from Crackerjack to jawbreakers to bubble gum and back to Crackerjack.

As they grow up, they never forget him, even though his store seems to dwindle in size once they have been away and his candy counter is no longer the most desirable siren in the world.

For kids "born in the store" there were good times and bad. Maybe you were tied in the yard sometimes when your mother was busy; maybe you were shy and the customers teased you; or maybe you were watched a little too

The store veranda is a place where generations of Canadian children have played . . . this one at Monteith in Northern Ontario.

closely . . . it wouldn't do for the merchant's children to run wild.

But if you wanted to build a snow fort or find the new kittens in the barn, or catch fireflies in a bottle, you had the customers' kids to help you. And there was no better place to play hide-and-go-seek than in the storehouses, attics and feedsheds connected to a country store. And on hot summer nights, you were allowed to sit up with the customers on the store veranda until the stars came out.

You were hardly ever lonely.

SUMMERTIME

*I*n spring, all you needed was a jacknife. You knew what tree was turning green, and you cut a couple of holes and you had a whistle. Or you made a slingshot.

In summer, we had the Ausable River three quarters of a mile to the west. About eight boys my age would go there to spend the whole day swimming. About half way down the sideroad, all our clothes would come off and they'd be hanging on fence posts all along the way. There were no people to watch and anyway we didn't care if there were.

On summer nights, boys and girls would sit on the store veranda, talking. Horses and buggies would be tied up there. A few times in summer, we would have ice cream which came in a huge, high wooden barrel. It would take two or three of us to wrestle the thing off the wagon. Inside, in the middle of all the ice and sawdust, there'd be a container with maybe two gallons of ice cream. Dad would put it in the cellar until the families would come in for Saturday night, and then there'd be ice cream for 5¢ a dish.

Cy Strange
Magwire, Ontario

STOREKEEPER'S TWINS

*T*he first year when I went back teaching, Bradley was three and the twins were two. We had the yard all fenced in. Bradley was shy and quiet, but the twins were never shy, never quiet. We found a lady, who was older and motherly, to look after them.

When the twins and Bradley would be out in the yard, the twins would decide to go exploring. They had found places where they could get under the fence. Then Mrs. Quinn would get all excited and she would get Albert, and the whole village would be looking for the twins. There was a creek to worry about.

One day, everybody in the village was out looking for them. A thunderstorm came up and they heard a clap of thunder and that got them scared. So they came running through the field, hand-in-hand, as hard as they could run. Everybody in the village was so glad to see them.

They loved people right from Day One. They used to stand at the fence near the gas pump. Every time they'd hear the gas bell, the two of them would run for the fence. I remember the ladies coming into the store laughing at what the twins had asked them. They would say, "Have you got your girdle on today?" Any new word that they liked the sound of, they would be trying it out.

Another lady came in and said, "You should see your boys out there."

I went out and found they had stripped. Neither one had a stitch of clothes on.

Doris Emond,
Camborne, Ontario

GONE TO THE STORE

*T*he first thing I can remember was getting through the fence to get to the store. Mother and Dad had a wire fence around our home to keep us wee kids in, and Dad and Mother thought they had all the holes blocked up that I couldn't get out. But I found a hole somewhere and got down to the store.

Dad used to have a couple of barrels of mixed candy there and tell people to help themselves. But if I was there, I'd give them a real big shovelful, so they had to stop me going down there.

Cecil Wasson,
Warsaw, Ontario

SMALL PEDDLERS

*O*ur father didn't have anything to do with the store. He was a sea captain and he would go to Australia or some place and be gone for eight or ten months at a time. He never came home on a regular schedule. If his ship came in to Halifax, he'd come home. He would just appear. He had a very loud voice . . . he'd open the door and yell and scare us all to death. It was very exciting, because he always brought us things that we didn't have, like oranges and sticks of sugar cane from the West Indies.

We were four boys and a girl. While my father was away, my mother had us all organized. When we were five and six, we had to put things on the shelves, draw kerosene, draw vinegar. People would send us jugs and we'd fill them. We had to get the wood and we had to carry water. Two of us boys together could carry a 100-pound bag of flour. Or chicken feed.

One or two days a week, we'd have to take the horse and buggy and peddle. There was a box on the back of the buggy and it had shelves. Mother would pack it full of all kinds of stuff, and we would go peddle this.

I'm the youngest boy. There were always two of us peddling. My mother used to send me because I was good at the figures. The older boy could handle the horse. To add 8¢ and 6¢ and 7¢ and 3¢ . . . that was my contribution to the business.

Joseph Ross,
Cape Negro, Nova Scotia

STORE DIPLOMACY

*S*ometimes you would catch them stealing and you wouldn't have the guts enough to tell them. One time when I was a boy helping in the store, I saw this fellow put two cuts of tobacco in his pocket. This was imported tobacco, cut on the end of the counter. I didn't have the guts to tell him to his face. So when I made out the bill, I just put it on the end of it.

He was shrewd enough. He looked up, "Gus, what's that?"
"That's for the two you put in your pocket."
"Oh. Oh, damn, I forgot all about those."

Gus Hayes,
Stephenville, Newfoundland

OLD JOHNNY, THE MILK AND McDONALD'S STORE

*W*hen I was four, Grandpa would hitch up the horse, Old Johnny, load the cans of milk on the milk wagon, put me up on the seat with a dime in my hand, give old Johnny a slap and off we would go down the road to the cheese factory.

The cheese-maker would take off the cans of milk while I

stayed on my seat. Then he would put the piece of paper in my shirt pocket (the receipt for the milk I'd brought). Old Johnny would start up by himself and take me to McDonald's store. I would get off now, go in with my dime and get my Coke. Old Johnny would wait exactly five minutes. By then I'd be back on and he would start off home.

That old horse could have taken the milk without me. My only purpose was to get that piece of paper for Grandpa. For that I got my dime and got to go to McDonald's store.

Allan Sheets,
Grant's Corners, Ontario

MILLIE AND ME

I'll tell you one that happened to me when I was a kid working at Marks' Store. Millie Johnson, she run the restaurant over there facing the railway track. She went to Mrs. Marks and asked if she thought I would drive her out to McRae's, because she wanted to get Mae McRae to help work in the restaurant. So when I came in to get my supper, I said, "Oh sure, I'll go." So I went down to the livery barn and got the livery team and we pulled out about nine o'clock.

It was late in the fall. We had to go north-east up to McRae's place, about 6 miles, and there was an open Hudson's Bay section to cross. And, of course, in those days there were no roads, just trails in every direction. So we got out there with no trouble at all.

But when we set out to come home about 11 o'clock, we could hardly see the horses. She said, "My goodness, what are we going to do?" I said, "Maybe the team will take us home." As a rule a horse will go home.

But that team didn't have no home. It was a livery team. Those horses kept goin' and goin' and goin' and goin'. Finally, I says to Millie Johnson, "You know something. I think we're lost; we should be home by now." It was starting to get daylight.

We were up in the Reid Hill District, way up in there. We came up to a big house on the top of this hill. So I said to Millie, "I'm going in to find out where we are." They were German people, but I finally made them understand.

He says, "You turn around, you go back the other way." By

that time it was starting to get daylight, so I could see just a little.

We pulled into the livery barn here just as the men were coming out to feed the horses. Boy, did they ever kid me about that. She was about 50 years old and I'd be about 17.

Harvey Beaubier,
Champion, Alberta

SUMMER STORM

*T*here would be a great quiet, a hush before the storm. We all stayed still on the store veranda in great expectation. Even the kittens were transfixed half way up the crabapple tree. But they felt the rain first, came dramatically to life and dashed for shelter under the store veranda. Slower, and reluctant to leave the new coolness, we humans moved inside, already splashed by big drops of rain.

Storekeepers' kids often went on to become storekeepers themselves. Mildred Swerdfeger grew up in this Morewood, Ontario store where her father, A.B. Allison, was the merchant.

For a time we just watched while the heavy drops pounded the veranda. Then the customers took their place by the counter, Mother leaned on the glass-top desk and started to write out the bills, and Dad collected the groceries in little separate piles for different customers.

Joyce or I might get sent to the storehouse for something, likely a big bag of puffed wheat. Out there you could hear the rain beating the tin roof and experience that almost ecstatic sense of security. There you could smell the special storehouse blend of cardboard and puffed cereal, and old cans of paint and coal oil. Outside the storehouse door, you could smell gasoline in the rain because Dad had just rushed out in an old coat to put in gas for someone who was in a hurry.

If there were other kids around on a night like this, we would slip out through the storehouse to play hide-and-seek in the feedshed. It had an upstairs or attic that was referred to simply as "over the feedshed". Up there you could hide behind the wallpaper shelves or among the stove-pipes stored in one corner. You could fit into an old piece of furniture in a dark corner, or you could climb into an old coat and disappear. The rain on the roof was very close here and you felt as snug and adventurous as a stowaway on an ocean-going ship.

Downstairs in the feedshed, you could hide in corners made by the piles of feed, or behind the scales, or under the attic stairs. If you didn't try it too often, you could fool the other kids by going through the shed-opening onto Dad's truck and hiding there.

Then the storm would peter out. Weary of hide-and-seek and unnaturally quiet, we would gather by the storehouse door to watch the summer sky begin to clear. The world would sit still, very still, except for the drip and the settling and sorting of the water. You could hear it running from the eaves down into the cistern. One of the kittens, subdued and almost reverent, would venture out from under the store veranda, picking up and placing down each small wet foot with meticulous care. The quiet kids in the storehouse door would all begin to laugh.

Enid Swerdfeger,
Glen Stewart, Ontario

CATCHING ON SLEIGHS

*W*hen the sleighs came into town for the farmers to do their shopping, the game was to catch a ride out . . . put your sled rope around the back runner and get hauled out for a while, then pick one that was coming in. Early in the day, it was hard to find one going out and, late at night, it was hard to find one coming in. So you had to be careful not to get too far out at night and have to walk back in the dark.

Florence Maynes,
Lemberg, Saskatchewan

COMMUNITY SUPPORT

*W*e had a farmer south-east of town who didn't believe in banks. He kept all his money in jars and he would bury these around the farm. He was quite wealthy, but very tight-fisted with his kids.

One day, the kids found a jar of this money. They came into the store and bought two bikes. They kept the bikes hidden in town and they would ride them in the bush. No one in the community would tell on them.

Maldwyn Hughes,
Lemberg, Saskatchewan

THE KIDS COME BACK

*I*t's a matter of being a part of the community. We've engaged in almost every sector of the community except actually ranching and farming . . . a lot of extra-curricular activity besides storekeeping. We've raised four children here and, at one time, these four sons were entirely away from town, and now three of them have seen fit to come back to this community. The fourth one will be retiring from the government of the Northwest Territories in four years, and he's seriously considering coming back here too.

John and Marion Green,
Pincher Creek, Alberta

STEALING MARSHMALLOW COOKIES

*T*here were four or five of us little girls, I wasn't going to school yet. In Taylor's store, around this pillar on the far side right against the wall, was this big rack full of these fabulous marshmallow cookies. But there was a crack, a little hole in one corner. So the kids all decided I was the tiniest, I could get my hand in there and get a cookie.

But they got the giggles because, when I got my hand in, the glass came down with a crack and here's Old Taylor waddling over. And, of course, my friends were all gone down Main Street, all but me. And my arm stuck. But when I did get away I had the one cookie. And I had to share all five bites with those kids outside.

Kay Jones,
Greenwood, British Columbia

Kids, bikes and country stores go well together. This attractive store is at Trout Creek on Ontario's Highway 11 near North Bay.

CHAPTER EIGHTEEN

IT WASN'T ALL ROSES

Katie MacLeod with her flowers at 92 in 1983. Since 1923 she has taken the good with the bad and still loves her Vernon River (P.E.I.) store, now run by her sons Lloyd and Don. (Katie does the books.)

Some days were bad. It was freezing cold behind the counter. The farmers were out of feed, and your truck refused to start. Or everyone in the family was down with flu, but someone had to wait on customers in the store. Or one of your children got hurt in the house, while you were busy in the store.

There were bills you couldn't collect and consequently debts you couldn't pay. There was the bone-weariness of hard work from seven to eleven. If you happened to be Chinese on the prairies, or a storekeeper who was teased by the kids, or both, there was loneliness and frustration and anger.

Sometimes the things that happened were funny, but you wouldn't see the humour at the time. Cleaning up molasses was not funny while you were doing it. Or trying to catch a runaway turkey. But looking back, most storekeepers laugh about the small disasters. Their point of view seems to say that you have to take the bad with the good. There is very little bitterness, just a rueful accounting of how it was on some days.

OUT THE BACK DOOR

When I was travelling on the road, I sold Chess Laing in Lockport a barrel of vinegar, 40 gallons. When I went back the next week, he ordered another barrel of vinegar. I said, "There's something wrong. You just had one last week."

"No," he said, "I need another barrel."

I said, "Well, you've sure sold vinegar!"

"I wouldn't say that I sold it. It all ran out the back door."

He had put a jug under the little spout and started the vinegar running, and went in to wait on more customers and never thought of it *again*. Until the next day. He lost the whole 40 gallons.

Stanley Smith,
Port Clyde, Nova Scotia.

JOBS I HATED

I surely did have jobs I hated. I *hated* filling kerosene and I hated pouring molasses into the jars with the tight yellow tops that wouldn't let air come through. And I hated getting Digby fish out of the box. They were dried and came in a little wooden box, and they were so smelly. You always had to go wash right after.

Customers never seemed to think. They would ask for their kerosene first, to put it into their sleigh, then would want dates or raisins. So it kept you washing your hands. There was no running water in the store. We kept a hand basin and a bucket of cold water in here.

Miriam Cousins,
Rose Valley, Prince Edward
Island

WALK BACK AGAIN

My husband, Harold, had the lake business . . . the store at McCracken's Landing on Stoney Lake . . . for a couple of summers. He liked it up there. I detested it!

All I could see, it was a place where you had to work extra hard. I wouldn't stay there, only on a bet. Once, I did stay there off and on for three weeks . . . that was the summer that

Jim was a year old and we were in a tent, and I never put in such a summer in my life.

One night it was so cold! I had taken plenty of bedding, but I was worried about Jim because he wasn't strong, born with a heart problem. He was sleeping on a cot slung up high . . . each boy had a cot, and I'll be hanged if I know what Hal and I slept on. But this night, I was so cold that I put on my clothes and wrapped Jim up, and started to walk home the six miles to Warsaw.

I think I walked about a half mile. Of course I just had to turn around and walk back again. I remember I was *so-oo* cold.

Beatrice Choate,
Warsaw, Ontario

The Choate store at McCracken's Landing, Ontario looked like this in the '20s and '30s. Here Beatrice Choate spent her first summer in a tent with her husband and four sons. "I never put in such a summer in my life!"

A TERRIBLE DAY

Dad never discussed business away from the store. If he'd had a terrible day, he'd come home and I would be chatting about school, Mother would be talking about Ladies Aid or the Missionary Society. "And how did you do, Dad?"

"Fine."

What was a terrible day? Well, maybe it would be wintertime, maybe forty below. One family had eight or ten children and for fun those kids liked to pee in the doorlock of the store. So Dad would go down in the morning to open the store, and find the lock frozen. That would start his day off.

Then there were the travellers coming in, the people not satisfied with lots of things, complaining. Then, of course, the bills; in those bad times it was awfully hard to collect the bills. And since it was a Co-op store, he had to account to his directors. And there would always be one or two directors . . . just like a knife . . . always finding fault.

Vera (Henry) Hughes,
Lemberg, Saskatchewan

The summer store at McCracken's Landing, Ontario depended on Stoney Lake for business.

The McCracken's Landing store as it looked in the 1950s. Stoney Lake has been a favourite haunt of fishermen, hunters, tourists and cottagers from Toronto for at least a hundred years.

NO PRIVACY FOR A GIANT

I'm a McAskill born, married to a McAskill. My grandfather was a brother of Angus McAskill, the giant who kept store at Englishtown. Angus was 7 feet, 9 inches and weighed 425 pounds. So I'm a grand-niece of the giant.

He died in 1863, and his store was gone before I was born. But there are stories about him. When he was selling tea, he would take the bulk tea in his hand and a handful would be a pound.

One time, men were trying to pull up a boat and he took hold of it to help and, for mischief, the men started pulling against him and he broke the boat in two.

He was a very quiet man. People used to go there to see him, and he knew they were going there just to see him. He would get up and walk around and then he'd disappear as if he felt embarrassed or shy, as if he wasn't normal.

Everyone always wanted to see him . . . even my little grandson. My son and his wife from Prince George were home just lately and have one little boy, and he wanted to see the giant's grave.

"Well, why don't you dig him up?" He was hollering, "Dig him up!" and at last he had to get a spanking. He was screeching. You could hear him on the other side of the island, "Why won't you dig him up?" His mother would say, "You know that nobody digs people up," but he wouldn't listen.

"Daddy could dig him up!"

Christine McAskill,
Little River, Nova Scotia

TEASING OLD ADAM

We would do some terrible tricks to Old Adam. He was so tight that he would cut a slice of bacon in half. So, on April Fool's Day, we used to go with the darndest list of everything that had to be weighed and cut and measured. And we'd say it was for Mrs. Cook . . . they had a real big family . . . and after he'd get it all measured and cut, we'd say "April Fool!"

He'd be wild. He'd phone my mother and she'd say, "Well, what would I do with all that stuff? If you are foolish enough to listen to these kids . . . you should know better after all these years." We had him weigh rice and brown sugar and cut bologna and bacon and cheese. We had a great time with Old Scrooge.

British Columbia

T.T. WONG

T. T. Wong: he was an older bachelor type at High River. Everybody remembers the jawbreakers he used to sell . . . and the licorice. I'm not sure how he made his living because he didn't have that much trade, mostly school kids that came in. All we knew him as, was T.T. Wong.

He stayed open until all hours of night. We used to get 15¢ to go to a hockey game just a block north of the store. If we had an extra nickel to spend, we went in afterwards and we could get a beautiful chocolate bar with nuts in it for 5¢ . . . that would be 75¢ now. One generation after another, as they went through their elementary grades, would pass by his place and buy jawbreakers or licorice or chocolate bars. It was the kids that kept him going.

It was a cold, drafty place, no central heat, just a pot-bellied stove in one area; in winter, he stood around with his back to it and stared out into space. In summer, kids would come along and throw in a jar full of grasshoppers and away they'd go. And he'd come roaring out of the place as fast as he could come. He never caught anybody.

He was not a very communicative fellow, quiet, never mixed with anyone. He died in the late '40s or early '50s, and it was three days before anyone found him in the back of his store. And that was the end of T.T. Wong.

Peter Pickersgill,
High River, Alberta

PULLING THIS WAY AND THAT

*M*y Dad just ran the store, he didn't own it. It was one of the earliest Co-op stores in Saskatchewan. Basically, Co-op was a farmers' organization. You bought in bulk, and things were cheaper. At the end of the year, the farmers got a refund, a percentage of everything purchased.

I hate to say this, but my Dad often didn't sell Co-op things, he liked other brands better. He could get away with that for a while. But in the latter years, I noticed the directors pulling this way and that. Dad was getting older, and I think maybe they wanted him out. They insisted that he sell all Co-op things. But Dad had had these independent salesmen for years and years and they would give him good deals . . . and they were his friends.

Vera (Henry) Hughes,
Lemberg, Saskatchewan

THE SKUNK

*O*ur basement under the store had a cistern in it, a big rectangular vat used to collect soft rain water. There was a window beside it and, in the spring of the year, Dad opened it to help dry out the dampness on the basement floor. A skunk came in and walked along the top edge of the cistern and settled himself on the bottom step of our basement stairs.

No one went downstairs for a while, but I remember us kids opening the cellar door and looking down on him sleeping there on the bottom stone slab. There was great discussion in the store how we should get him out. Some had theories about moth balls, which skunks didn't like, or about meats, which skunks did like, for luring him out. Others offered to shoot him. The consensus of opinion was that we should take a big rock and drop it on him. My mother refused.

Meanwhile, Dad had hopefully put a plank from the cistern to the window to make it easier if Mr. Skunk should want to go. Finally, one day he did.

Enid Swerdfeger,
Glen Stewart, Ontario

CLOSE TO THE BONE

*T*he bad thing I remember was slicing T-bone steak with the handsaw. The Hôtel St. Jovite bought all their steak here. So they phone for the weekend, "We want 60 T-bone steaks." The store was not insulated well, so in the winter, the meat was frozen every morning. It is very tough working with frozen meat . . . very cold for the fingers. When we finish cutting the T-bone steaks with the handsaw, all the fingers were all in blood, because the saw jumps all ways when you begin to cut the bone.

Guy Richer,
St. Jovite, Quebec.

MOLASSES ALL THE WAY

*M*olasses was rationed during the war, but we had quite a big quota because we sold a lot before the war. Father had been a boat builder — during the First World War he built lifeboats. Then he built a small store and enlarged it. Then we started selling to other stores at Cape Island and Barrington, and got into the wholesale business. We had a bigger quota for molasses than any of the wholesalers in Yarmouth. And molasses was the biggest headache we had during rationing.

It came in such big quantities: a puncheon would be 100 gallons, a tierce would be about 50 gallons. We didn't know who to give the barrel to. If we'd give it to one person, the next person was mad. A lot of these little stores could sell a puncheon of molasses every two or three weeks. People put molasses in everything they cooked — molasses cakes, jelly rolls, baked beans. And they always had a jug of it on the table.

Then we lost one shipload coming in. Torpedoed. We had already paid for it, but then the insurance company paid us.

Another headache was when we'd spill molasses in our own store. In winter, it was so cold, so slow. We'd put the measure under it and go back inside to wait on someone else while it was running. Different times we'd go out and you couldn't ever see the gallon measure because it was under a pyramid of molasses. Talk about a mess of goo. An awful job to clean it up.

Then there was that hot, hot day in July when we were hauling molasses down from Yarmouth by truck. The trouble was they didn't open the vent on the puncheon. The molasses got working in the heat and blew the head out of it, and kept running out the closed body of the truck. The driver didn't know it.

A hundred gallons in that puncheon. Awful mess in the truck when he got here. And there was molasses on the road all the way from Pubnico to Port Clyde.

Edward Stoddard,
Port Clyde, Nova Scotia

CHAPTER NINETEEN

THEN THE CARS CAME

Many Canadians over 70 remember events by which car they had at the time. If Dad were driving the Model T Ford, then that happened the same year Gladys was born. But if he had a Chev, then that train wreck must have been in 1931.

Canadians over 80 vividly remember the day they saw their first car or had their first ride in one. They can describe the weather that day and what the driver of the automobile was wearing.

Storekeepers welcomed the cars at first. Automobiles could bring people to the stores faster and more often. But it soon became apparent they they could also take them farther away. The rural patchwork quilt that featured a store and church and school, blacksmith shop, cheese factory and mill every three or four miles, would be tattered and torn by these fiery demons of speed.

Ian Darrah of Glassville, New Brunswick recalls being told in the 1930s, "They're gonna build some nice roads by your place, and the people are gonna go right by to the supermarkets." Ian likes to point out that he is still there and his store still looks the same, although his business and his customers have changed a great deal over the years. And most of his fellow storekeepers to the north, east, south and west are gone.

Cars, more than any other single factor, changed the rural way of life in Canada. They changed and threatened, and sometimes destroyed the country store.

Here at Grand Bend, Ontario, on Lake Huron, the cars have come and life will never be so quiet again.

DAD'S FIRST CAR

*I*t was a 1930 car. Dad took possession of it in town and got a brief lesson, and pointed it toward home. The people who saw him coming said he must have floored the gas pedal; it was a gravel road and the gravel was all flying out behind.

He got it home all right. Then we all got after him to take us for a drive. Mother got in too. We sat there for a long time, because he couldn't remember how you got it started. Then when he got it started, he couldn't recall what to do next. He tried putting it in gear without the clutch, then he remembered about the clutch.

Then he floored it again, and we took off down the lane. Very suddenly! He was going too fast, so what did he do about it? He put it in reverse. It didn't ruin the engine either because he had it right to the floor. He went roaring backward up the lane with us inside all shook around. When he got it stopped, he let it sit right there in the lane for three days until he got up his nerve to drive again.

After we got the car, we were much more mobile. With horses, St. Walburg was a place we could get to only on weekends; with the car we could get in to shop any day of the week. Spruce Lake and Loon Lake and Paradise Hill were new places we could get to now . . . the car opened up a whole new world.

Walter Tarasuk,
St. Walburg, Saskatchewan

MAGWIRE

*T*he store I grew up in was called Magwire. Magwire was a store and post office near Exeter, east from Lake Huron. It was on a sideroad, and when the '20s and '30s came and people had cars, they left it behind and it just sort of dwindled away. Now Magwire is no longer on the map.

Cy Strange,
Magwire, Ontario

THEN THE CARS CAME

When I was a girl, I worked in the Keene Emporium for four years. It's gone now. Oh, we sold everything! Harness, linoleum, hardware. We used to have a keg of salted herrings outside the door in rock salt . . . 5¢ each.

There was an upstairs in the store where we sold boots and shoes and men's overalls and men's underwear, those big woollen underwear suits, and work shirts. And above that was another room which was the Masonic Lodge. Then the great big warehouse out the back where they sold paint and coal oil and eavestroughs and pumps. Sugar by the hundred and flour by the hundred.

Books of wallpaper . . . you had to order your wallpaper. Also men's suits, you could buy material for suits out of those big "Hobberlin" books. When I was there, the suits came made up, but earlier than that, they used to keep a tailor in the store and they made up suits right there. Suits were $15 or $18 or $20, extra pants $3 to $4.

And we sold dishes. And bread. Bread used to come in wooden boxes with just slats on the side of it. And it wasn't wrapped. But they were lovely big brown loaves. A man used to draw them down from the train to the store with a team of ponies every morning.

Along with the trains, river travel was important at Keene. I remember when the steamer *Rainbow* used to go up the river to Peterborough. We used to go up and spend the day in town. It called at every little stop along the way. And we used to go on Moonlight Excursions. They'd call at the end of our line, and if it was shallow they'd put a board out to the scow. They used the scow, pulled behind the *Rainbow*, for dancing. There were lots of people could play the violin then.

Then the cars came. My dad didn't learn to drive, but he had a man come down from Duffus' Garage in Peterborough where he bought the car. And he stayed for two days teaching me to drive. We lived right over a big hill, so I had to learn to drive up that big hill. I was supposed to teach my dad to drive, but he didn't learn for years after. I had to go to all the Farmers' Union Meetings and the Cheese Factory Meetings, and sit out in the car while my dad went to meetings.

And the roads were so narrow and the horses all shy, and they'd jump off the road when you had to meet them. We

This store at Heidelberg, Ontario, in the heart of Mennonite country, recalls the days before cars came. The store has a rich history of serving these industrious German settlers who have prospered in spite of religious taboos which prohibit modern farming methods and automobiles.

never drove the car in the winter . . . put it up on blocks. In the fall, my dad and I took the car all apart and cleaned all the motor, and replaced anything that needed replacing. Many the time we patched tires . . . you'd take the tire off and patch the rubber tubing inside. We had a manual, but we had it wore out.

Nobody drove their cars in the winter. The roads weren't ploughed at all.

Alice Davidson,
Keene, Ontario

BEFORE THE CARS CAME

*W*e had a girl who worked in the store, and every Wednesday she used to go down this road here and call on every house to the lower end of Port Saxon, three or four miles. Not all the houses would be on the road, sometimes a half mile off. If they wanted a gallon of molasses or kerosene or vinegar, she would set the jug out at the head of the road, and when we came to pick her up, we'd pick up the jugs, too. There would be times when she would carry them along with her, if there weren't too many, then she would catch the train to come back.

That was about the only way these people could get served, because they had no cars, no horses, sometimes not even a boat.

Edward Stoddard,
Port Clyde, Nova Scotia

THROUGH A FELT HAT

We started the store in 1921. Everything was in bulk. You'd have to dig out figs and raisins, weigh everything out. Horseshoe nails in kegs (you'd wreck your hands on those). We had coal oil in a tank in the basement and had to pump it up. We even had big 300-pound barrels of corn syrup. There'd be more messes of corn syrup to clean up!

When cars first came, gasoline was in drums. That was in the early '20s. You would pump it into gallon measures. Then you would put a funnel in the car and strain the gas through a felt hat.

Lily Hudson,
Boulter, Ontario.

THREE GALLONS

In the first 20 years, cars didn't make any difference . . . or even helped the business, because people came from more distant places. And I had the gas pumps; I was the only one that had gas here. The first pump I had was a blind pump. There was just a needle on it, up to five gallons. Then the glass pumps came in and you would pump up 10 gallons.

I would be bothered an awful lot at night; after midnight, there would be somebody coming from the north or from Sydney and running out of gas. So at last, I would pump up three gallons of gas, and then I'd lock the handle on it so if anybody was stuck, let them take the three gallons. So they wouldn't bother me.

I would see it empty in the morning, but I never lost any of it. They would always send me the money . . . from Sydney, New Waterford, Glace Bay. And I even made money on it. Gas was 33¢ a gallon but instead of a dollar, there would be a two-dollar bill in the letter.

A.J. Morrison,
North River Bridge, Nova
Scotia

DON'T GO TOO FAST

*B*usiness in St. Jovite started to get good in 1950 and very fast after that. I bought the business from Father in 1951, just when the unions in Montreal were giving more time and more money, so the employees were able to come up every Friday night, spending a lot of money here on Saturday and Sunday, building little shacks to fish and hunt and swim and ski. Then, a few years after that, the shacks were quite good, so they were able to come very often, and now they come every weekend, 52 weeks a year. At first they came by train, but after the war, the good roads came and then the cars came.

Father died at 55; did not live to see the store succeed. He had lost much money in 1932. Mother's father had a little bit of money and he had a friend, Mr. Paquette, who saved my father's store, lent him about $1500.

But Father stayed poor all his life. I remember one day after Labour Day, my mother asking my father, "Where is all our money. We worked the whole summer and we have no money."

My father told my mother, "I spend $100 on the shed and altogether I spend about $400, that's all." Of course, he had a payment to make of $665 on the store. So after that he makes $400 for the whole summer and he wonders where the $400 is gone. He has nothing left. He works for nothing. And after Labour Day, business is very quiet . . . nothing more.

Father saw just the beginning of big business. He couldn't believe that. When I bought new refrigerators and automatic checkouts in 1953 or 1954, he couldn't believe it. He said, "Don't go too fast my little boy! Don't go too fast."

Guy Richer,
St. Jovite, Quebec

A CAR BEFORE ITS TIME

When my father came to trade on the west coast of
Newfoundland, it was all done by boat. Then around 1900, they
built the railway. The workers got one dollar a day . . . and
cook your own meals on your shovel, fry your fat pork or
bacon that way. They built narrow-gauge, three-and-a-half feet
instead of four feet wide.

Then the cars. I've got the oldest licence on the
Newfoundland west coast, got it in 1919 in Detroit. I drove
Model T Fords from Detroit to North Sydney. I would buy them
for $260, pay a 30% duty, bring them to North Sydney and sell
them for $1000. I wouldn't bring the cars to Newfoundland. No
good bringing them here. No roads to drive them on. Well, we
had dirt roads, but no bridges. You couldn't get anywhere
without bridges.

Bishop Power had the first car in St. George's. His brother,
Tony, made a lot of money on land deals in Ontario and he sent
him this car. Big expensive car. But he never ran it. There were
no roads to run it on.

They gave us kids a day off from school to haul it up to the
barn with a block and tackle, and it stayed there until he died
shortly after. Then his brother came and took the car to St.
John's.

It never was driven. I don't know if anybody even knew
how to operate a car in those days. The hens roosted on it at
one time there.

Gus Hayes,
Stephenville, Newfoundland

DAVY TUCKER'S CAR

My uncle had the store at Indian River. My mother
remembers when she was a young married lady, going to the
store with the horse and buggy to shop. And as they got over
the brow of the hill, they could see this car approaching. And
their horse was very mettlesome. And Mother says to Aunt
Mary, "Oh dear, I hope we don't meet on the culvert, "it's not
very wide."

They tried to hold the horse back, but they couldn't. So
they did . . . they met right on the culvert. And poor Davy

Tucker's car went off on one side. And he was just in a fury. And Aunt Mary, who trained for a nurse, said, "Are you hurt, Mr. Tucker? Are you hurt, Mr. Tucker?"

And he yelled, "Sh–ut Up!"

Muriel Fife,
Indian River, Ontario

ONE SOUVENIR

I was a little boy and Louis St. Laurent came home to the store with a big car and a big driver who was a negro. I never see one before. And in 1912 or 1913, we don't see many cars. He drive a big Reo car. "How would you like to have a ride?"

By Gad, we jump in the car! We did have a ride! We all remember that. Big chauffeur and big Reo car. We like the car, but we like the chauffeur, too. They both were new.

That's one souvenir I get from Louis St. Laurent.

Joseph Denis,
Compton, Quebec

CLOSING THE STORE

*Y*ou just couldn't make a living in the store in the 1950s. By that time everybody had cars and gas, and the stores in town had such beautiful bargains, you could not compete with them. So the people would gaily drive by here, get all their nice groceries, come home, maybe pick up a quart of milk here. And charge it! So it just got impossible.

We decided to just ease out. Nobody wanted to buy a store. We owned the building and we kept it as a home and my husband turned to carpentry.

When I think of all the good things that went to the dump. Of course, all the patent medicines . . . Dr. Chase's Pink Pills for Pale People and Lydia Pinkham's Compound For Women Born Without a Bust . . . we shovelled them all out, a dead loss. But the canned goods you could use up. Harry Horne's Pudding Powders we used for years. Canned meats and soups and spices. I think my daughters are still using some of those spices. We just let the stock dwindle down and didn't restock the store.

Of course, the neighbours all said, "They're going broke."

We weren't going broke, but we would have if we had stayed on!

Jean (Weir) Drimmie,
Lang, Ontario

SUCH A FEW YEARS

*T*he store was one of these things that came and went in such a few short years. And then Finnie started to disappear. And now the highway goes straight through where it used to be and there's nothing there.

The station went; they closed it when they didn't have as many trains going through. Then the elevators went. When people got cars, they didn't depend on the train. When times got better after the war, they would go to the bigger towns for entertainment, go to doctors and dentists, and get their groceries there. Then the small little hamlets like Finnie were not needed anymore.

I can see the store there yet, with the horses and sleighs or horses and buggies coming in, and people hitching them up to the hitching rail. And later, the cars and trucks. When we first started, it was nearly all horses. In 10 years, it went through that whole period.

Corine (McGarry) Stillborn,
Finnie, Saskatchewan

Ian Darrah's store in Glassville, N.B. has survived the coming of cars and superhighways and super-markets to remain a popular place of business.

CHAPTER TWENTY

FROM YESTERDAY TO TOMORROW

Louis St. Laurent grew up in this ▷ house and store in Compton, Quebec, where his father, Jean-Baptiste Moise St. Laurent, settled as storekeeper in 1878. While Louis became Prime Minister of Canada, his brother Maurice took over the store. Marc St. Laurent, son of Maurice, gave up the store in 1969 because Parks Canada wanted to restore it as a historic site. Visitors can see both the store and house as they looked in the early 1900s.

Old storekeepers hate to quit. The store itself is a living thing, and to leave it, sell it or . . . horror of horrors . . . close it down, is a painful act. So some of them hang on until they fall "a heap on the floor". •Sometimes the heap gets up and faces the facts. Sometimes it is too late to get up.

Times do change and stores do disappear. The cars have come and the supermarkets dominate and the computer-robotic age changes everything. Many old stores and old storekeepers have been left on a sideroad, or on a railway track where trains no longer run. The story of country stores is sometimes a story of their disappearance.

But there is a new breed of storekeeper: sons, daughters, successors to the "salty old breed". They have all the determination and drive of the old pioneers, but they have also new marketing techniques, metric cash registers and computerized purchasing systems. They say loud and clear, individually and through their federations, that the independent country store is not dead. Their conventions, which your typical "old storekeeper" would have called "pure nonsense" or "a waste of time", allow them to share and

compare ways of competing against the national chains.
Getting together also gives them the support of other human
beings struggling against the same odds.

They are now getting good help from their wholesalers.
They are learning all the tricks of the supermarket, and their
stores have some advantages the supermarkets don't have.
And most of them love the life they are living.

OUR OWN PATHS

When Father stopped taking orders around the lakes, Grandfather told him, "If you do that you are going to lose your store." The next year, Father had his biggest year so far.

Now I and my four sisters own the store. One year ago now, we children decided to stop all deliveries with the truck, and Father was saying, "Not sure you gonna make a good move." And this reminded me of what Grandfather said when Father stopped delivering to the lakes in 1947.

We want to follow our fathers, but we want to make our own paths.

Mario Richer,
St. Jovite, Quebec

GENERATIONS

My grandfather had a really general store at Montcerf in northern Quebec. He used to buy flour by the carload and a carload of pork in the barrel. Molasses used to come in a 40- or 60-gallon drum. And maple syrup and corn syrup. He was supplying the lumber jobbers up in the Gatineau.

He was a personal friend of Sir Wilfrid Laurier. In 1917, two years before Laurier died, I saw him in my grandfather's living room. I was seven years old. What I remember is that my cousin and I came into the living room, and we would be noisy and my grandfather told us to "cool it". I remember Laurier's white hair, the way it was curled at the back. Grandfather was a well-to-do businessman and I think they were trying to get him into politics. But Grandfather was a little deaf, so he didn't go into politics.

My dad took our family to Larder Lake, Ontario in 1922, before the railway came. In the summer of 1923, we used to see the airplane from Haileybury going to what is now the mining centre of Noranda. It would fly up the Ontario-Quebec border and then we could see it go east over the north-east arm of Larder Lake. We could see it come back and, by watching how long it took, we could figure out that it would be inside the Quebec border maybe 30 or 40 miles. That fall, we learned that they had discovered Noranda. The following year, there was a railway built from Larder Lake to Cheminis on the Ontario-Quebec border.

That's when my dad sold his pool room and barbershop at Larder Lake, and built the store at Cheminis in 1924. It was a boom town! We supplied a lot of prospectors. If they were not going too far, they would buy 16 loaves of bread. Otherwise, they would buy flour and baking powder, beans, raisins, prunes and Borden's canned milk, tea, coffee and sugar.

In the Depression, I finally got work at Kirkland Lake, then worked in a hardware store at Larder Lake. But I wanted a place of my own. I came south to look and found this store at Camborne. I came here on a Monday morning, January 5th, 1952. I had lunch with Mr. Maguire and asked him what he wanted and I wrote it down. I got home up north on Thursday morning and told my wife. She said, "That sounds all right." So I called Mr. Maguire and said, "It's a deal."

He said, "I can depend on your word?"

I said, "Yes, I'll be there Tuesday."

We landed here on Tuesday the 14th and were in business on the 15th. It was just a gentleman's agreement. They were moving out while we were moving in. There were no papers signed. The following Wednesday we went to the lawyers and I paid the Maguires.

Our business has been steady for 30 years. I like the way it is, a one-man business. There's no pressure. I meet a lot of nice people. I have time to talk to people. Sometimes they give me advice; sometimes I give them advice. It's a good way of life. It's a beautiful way of life.

Albert Emond,
Camborne, Ontario

THE INDEPENDENTS WILL FLOURISH

*A*s president of the Canadian Federation of Retail Grocers from 1977 until last year, I got to know Canada and the food industry quite well. The independent grocers have really been sat on by the big corporates . . . with the help of government. The government didn't give a damn about the small independent. The big corporates came in and they just smothered the small independent stores.

Towns store in 1936.

The P.G. Towns store at Douro, Ontario, built in 1896, as it appeared in 1909.

The old wholesalers . . . National Grocers in particular . . . did nothing to help the independent grocers. They were like sleeping giants and have just now wakened up. All of a sudden they have come to life, but if they had done this 20 years ago, the whole situation would have changed in Ontario.

The old wholesaler knew how to be nice to the storekeeper, but the storekeeper didn't know the best ways to order, to manage, to promote and to sell. The big corporates learned how to, fast. This is one thing our federation tries to teach store-keepers . . . you've got to smarten up, you've got to study, you've got to take courses, you've got to use computers.

However, right now in 1983, the big chains are just being throttled by the unions. Wages are now running 20% of their gross dollar. A cashier can get $23 000. So here the independents have an advantage. The chains are asking supervisors to get more and more work out of their employees.

That causes dissension, and eventually they will call a strike. And that'll be just great, because then the independents will just flourish.

Ken Gadd,
Peterborough, Ontario

LET ME OUT OF HERE

*B*iscuits came in 27-pound wooden boxes. When you opened soda biscuits made in Newfoundland, they were crisp, delicious. Even after being up in the store loft for four or five months, they'd be good. Sugar came in butts, 300 pounds. Beans came in 100-pound sacks. Rolled oats came in barrels. Flour came in 196-pound barrels.

If some of the people who died a few years ago came back now and realized that the only flour you could buy was in a

Towns store as it looks today.

The P.G. Towns store at Douro, Ontario has undergone several changes since 1896 but still has managed to retain a special flavour and the faithful allegiance of its customers.

2 1/2-pound bag, but you bought your bread at a bakery at $1.05 a loaf, they'd say, "Let me go! Quick!"

They'd say, "You mean you're my son, and you do that?"

Herb Gillett,
Twillingate, Newfoundland

THINGS ARE GETTING BETTER

I worked for Loblaws for two or three years in the meat department and it was cold . . . I had trouble with arthritis in my hands . . . so my brother-in-law had the store here for sale. Before that it was closed, until he opened it eight years ago. Now we've been here five years.

Things are getting better for the country stores. We are more competitive now; we deal with Oshawa Wholesale and our prices now are the same as I.G.A. and Food City.

We run it as a family business. We have four kids and they help on the weekend and in summertime. So the money doesn't go out of the house; it stays right in the business. In summertime here, we almost double our business, with all the tourists.

The Oshawa Wholesale Group is fantastic. They are very, very good. I needed a new scale when we went metric and they bought it through the organization. I had to pay for the shelving, but not the labour; they were here with three men for two days and they set it all up for me. The scale itself cost me $1700.

Things are going well. Every year we fix up something. At Loblaws, they did the thinking for you; you followed orders. Here, it's just the opposite. We're happy with the store business. Hope to stick with it.

*Joe Vandermeulen,
Keene, Ontario*

SIGN OF THE TIMES

*S*IGN is the acronym for Support Independent Grocers Now. It is an organization which we put together because, in Western Canada, we see the independent grocer, both the small-town and medium-sized markets, going by the wayside because of the huge corporate. In Western Canada, we have one chain,

Safeway, which is a monopoly now. On the federal level, big business gets to the government. So we have to put pressure on our Alberta government to give the independent grocer an advantage.

I guess the country store, as we know it, is not going to be there anymore . . . it will be there in a different fashion. There'll be fewer of them, they'll be very smart operators. But they certainly can do it because there are people that like the country store atmosphere.

And the convenience of having a store close to you. The storekeeper has to recognize this and not try to compete with the big stores, because, even if you are competitive, they are not going to believe you. You might as well get your price and enjoy it and help your customers enjoy it.

Supermarkets make it appear that they are more competitive, by different mark-ups on different products. This is what the customer concentrates on . . . Heinz ketchup, their favourite coffees. Whereas the smaller grocers will make 20% right across the board, instead of 25%. So the illusion is there that they are higher-priced. In fact, they probably are a little, but not enough to warrant driving 20 miles.

I used to fly in the Air Force and I found that extremely exciting. When I got out, by chance I got into the grocery business. I find now that it is probably the most exciting business . . . fast-moving, hard, but rewarding. It has been rewarding to us and I know a lot of grocers who have found it profitable and rewarding.

It's very much worth protecting.

Wally Protsack (president of SIGN),
Rocky Mountain House, Alberta

A HEAP ON THE FLOOR

I took over the store from a brother in 1940. Times had changed a lot from the rich days of shipping grain and apples and butter from Prince Edward County. But I saw a new angle. I had a farm and I could turn it to beef, slaughter the beef and sell it in the store. I put in a deep freeze and a meat-cutting room with power saw and meat grinder, and went into the butcher business. For the next 20 years, our Country Store at

Rednersville hummed with business. I had people coming from Belleville and Trenton to fill their freezers with our beef. Chickens, too. I would have two bushels of chickens ready every Saturday night.

On summer weekends, we used to hang 15 — 20 stalks of bananas across the front of the veranda. We specialized in meat and fresh fruit . . . bananas, apples, tomatoes . . . which brought the people in, then they bought everything else as well.

We operated the store and farm and raised 11 children. I kept up the pace until one night in 1960, when I fell in a heap on the floor. It was 11 o'clock at night. I reached for a can of paint on a top shelf and blacked out. When I came to and got up, I said, "You fool, it's time to quit."

Bernard Redner,
Rednersville, Ontario

A STORE OF HIS OWN

My father was a farmer and he bought me a farm, and I ran it for four years, but I got dissatisfied with it. I had been away to school and had some training, so I sold the farm and bought the store in 1926.

Father was never too happy farming, so he left the farm and came with me in the store. Oh, he loved the store. Talked to people; had a great time. There was a little store came for sale in Tryon when he was about 75, and he said to me, "I believe I'll go and buy that store, and I'll go up there and run it."

I said, "All right, we'll buy it." So we bought the store. He did fine on his own. Of course, I supplied him with all the stock. He ran that store for 10 years, until he died very suddenly at 85.

Brent Wood,
Crapaud, Prince Edward Island

I'M ALMOST SEVENTY

A lot of people tell me now that I'm almost 70, "Why don't you retire? Why don't you close the door?"

I say, "All my friends are here; at age 70 you don't make friends where you go." And I tell people I can't live anywhere as cheap as I do here. My taxes on this building are roughly

$400. I get part of that back in my income tax for my business. Where can I live on $200 or $300 a year? You can't live anywhere for $300 a year.

Our customers are local people; they've been with us ever since Dad was here. Now it's more of a hobby. We close at six o'clock every day of the week. The few bucks we make here keep us happy. We keep the community going.

There's a lady here, her husband's not very well, can't drive a car; she has no way of getting out, she does all her business here. If I lock the door, what's she gonna do? And she's not the only one. There's dozens of them like that, depending on me.

Bill Mason,
Makinak, Manitoba

WHAT ELSE?

*H*enry H.W. Reimer . . . when they were about to tear down that store, he came day by day and sat there and looked at the store of days gone by. He had been in that store all his life; he had been trading with the people from very young until in his 80s.

First, they sold everything out of the building. He had kind of a platform so high, which he sat on so he could look all over the store. A big building it was, 160 by 40 feet. They had sold out everything except the cash register and the safe and his books. And they had a habit, when selling out, of getting some supplies so that the people would come again. And one thing they kept to the very end, and kept it fresh, that was frozen fish.

That night, when I came into the Reimer store, the walls were all bare, even those long step ladders that had rails along the ceiling . . . all gone. There was nothing left. The floor and the walls were bare. There was only a bag of fish in the shed outside of the heated quarters, and that was all they had that night when a customer came in. And they had only newspaper to wrap the fish up. And when this fellow bought some fish and he wrapped it up, Henry H.W. said, "And what else would you like?" As he had done for 80 years.

This customer said, "What else? You got nothing else!"

John Reimer,
Steinbach, Manitoba

OVER THE RAINBOW

Grandfather was a capitalist. He owned half of Warsaw. As well as the store, he had a flour and feed mill, houses and land in the area. There was a sawmill there too, and he was involved in that. At one time, he had a lot of money, but that wasn't enough, he was gonna be a millionaire . . . so he lost all his money in the stock market. About 1910, I believe.

When Grandpa fell on bad times, he'd be past middle-age. He died at 96 in 1939, so he'd be over 65 when this happened. But he didn't lament. There were no tears shed . . . well, there might have been internally. But it wasn't a tragedy, so to speak.

When he was 90-some years of age, he lived with us for about six months, when we were at Warminster Cheese factory. In those days, they gave them a $10 old age pension. And Grandpa used to say to my dad, "Ralph, if I just had a buggy or a wagon, I know I could go out and travel around and turn this money into a lot of money. He wanted . . . at 90-some years of age . . . to get going again.

He never gave up hope, always figured, "I'll do well, I'll get by." Some people get up in years and their life is gone. But not Grandpa Wasson. It was all just waiting over the rainbow there for him!

Neil E. Wasson,
Warsaw, Ontario

CHAPTER TWENTY-ONE

HANDS ACROSS THE COUNTER

The relationship between merchant and customer was often close and personal, even when one or the other was quite unusual. Reaching across the counter in all their eccentricity, they forged a bond that sometimes lasted decades. Mrs. Fennell of Cherry Valley store, in Ontario, tells of a man who came to shop every Friday night without fail for 30 years. Elsie Chapman of Lac du Bonnet, Manitoba, recalls taking in furs for an old fur buyer, "I think for 75 years." Guy Richer of St. Jovite, Quebec says, "Mr. Wheeler is like a grandfather to me. His father was a customer here in 1925."

Every storekeeper has a long list of valued customers without whose patronage his business would not have flourished. Then there are others whose personalities made them valuable in terms of entertainment. These are the customers you can't forget.

Customers also have their stories and vivid portraits of merchants they will always remember. They remember that they were fat or thin or wore jumbo sweaters cut off at the elbow, or smoked cigars or read the Bible between customers. Most clearly and fondly remembered are merchants who "helped them out" when they had hit rock bottom financially. Harvey Beaubier recalls old R.B. Allen, the storekeeper in Stavely, Alberta. "That fellow staked, oh, all kinds of people for grub, and he'd carry them over another year. Otherwise a lot of people never could have stayed."

The P.G. Towns store at Douro, Ontario, after 88 years of business, has a reputation for fair-dealing and scrupulous honesty. A man, on a bus from Toronto to Peterborough, told me how he left Douro and came back after 11 years. When he went into Towns General Store, Joe Towns reached across the counter and handed him 27¢. "Here," he said, "I over-charged you this much last time you were in."

"Eleven years ago! He remembered that 27¢ for 11 years!"

Some storekeepers become legends in their times. Some customers become immortalized by the unusual shape of their lives or the good deeds they did, the pranks they played or the stories they told. What they shared, what they still share in the country store, forms a strong thread . . . colourful, elastic and long-wearing . . . in the fabric of Canadian life.

In High River, Alberta, clerks at the Little Bow Trading Company served customers across this elegant rounded counter.

ALL DEAD

*T*his cash register was new in 1913, shiny gold metal. Now the metal on one side is all blackened. Our store is wide, so the dry-goods counter was too far away, and the customers liked to sit here on the grocery counter. There was room enough for several customers and their groceries too.

They're all dead! Them that used to sit on the counter and scratch their matches to light their pipes. All dead! My wife wanted to try to clean it, but I told her not to. It's worth $300 more with them scratch marks on it.

Lara and Hans Tergesen,
Gimli, Manitoba

CHECKERS

*M*y grandfather was the best checker player in the Lakehurst area. I have the checker board from the store and the squares are actually worn right off in the centre section, so you can't tell the black from the red, there was so much checkers played on it.

He always got the checker board out on Saturday night. Saturday was really a big night. Everybody came to the store, and a lot of the younger men sat around and they'd buy cookies and bologna and cheese. After everybody had done their shopping, the young men stayed and played checkers. They had benches then in front of the counters, and Grandfather had a step-thing built to get up to the top shelves, so he used to lean that against one counter, and whoever was playing checkers with him sat on a bench on the other side of it.

Beth McMaster,
Peterborough, Ontario

MUSKRATS IN THE SWAMP

*W*hile teaching school in a remote northern community, I encountered one of the most interesting storekeepers that I have ever met. Abie Sanioskioffi was like a little king in the community. Many of the people worked for him, one way or

another . . . ice-fishing in winter, lumbering or driving huge truck loads of lumber across the frozen lake in winter. There was no RCMP stationed in the village, so it was the storekeeper who kept order, helped settle fights, or refused to give more liquor to someone who had obviously had enough.

When they were "broke", he would let them charge things at his store, on the strength of their promise to pay when the Family Allowance cheques came in. Since he was also the postmaster, he knew when the cheques arrived. That day he would sit on the counter, playing his accordian and singing lustily, "I'm Looking Over a Four-Leaf Clover", or doing his Jimmy Durante imitations. After a while, he would hand out the cheques, making sure that all charge accounts were paid in the process.

Or a trapper might come to him, asking for a grubstake to buy traps and supplies for his trapline, promising to repay him in muskrat skins. These accounts he referred to as his "Muskrats in the Swamp".

He seemed to thrive on the isolation and hardships. Three times his store was destroyed by fire but, eternal optimist that he was, three times he rebuilt it.

My last memory of him is my final trip out to "civilization" . . . bouncing along a narrow, rutted trail through the swamp, while he went through his repertoire of songs. Then a hair-raising journey across the lake, the ice covered with water, and the cracks in the ice widening before our eyes, while he sang his favourite songs . . . "I'm Looking Over a Four-Leaf Clover".

Walter Dziadow,
Arborg, Manitoba

The old store counter was the meeting place of merchant and customer. Made of wood, polished by the hands of generations, it was often ornate with cash registers and brass scales, brown paper racks and coffee grinders. This is John Dazé's general store in Arnprior, Ontario. The customers are Messrs. Strand and Dack.

A LEGEND IN HIS TIME

Herman Kavelman came here to New Dundee, south of Kitchener, Ontario from Germany in 1899 when he was 16. He became a clerk in Jacob Kriesel's store at a $30-a-year salary, plus board. At the end of the first year, Kriesel raised his salary to $40 and bought him a new suit. By 1910, Kavelman had bought the store and married Kriesel's sister.

He was a natty dresser, always drove the newest type of car. He could pull people's teeth or fix people's watches or clocks. He was a skilled photographer who could put photos on ladies' fingernails (pictures of boyfriends were popular for local dances).

When he sold out in 1971, the auction lasted for more than a week . . . people flew in . . . the place was filled with treasures and antiques. An American couple bought the old store and re-named it "The Emporium". In 1975, we bought both the store and the adjoining Kavelman's Hall. We've continued and expanded the Emporium theme.

But there's a lot of the Herman Kavelman era still here. High starched collars and sailor hats. Our old pine counters, the nooks and crannies where he repaired watches or hung hardware and harness, or stored flour and dried apples. The file boxes he frugally made out of old cigar boxes. He drilled holes in the floor to let the water out when the roof leaked. He was old by this time and not about to roof the place for some future owner's benefit.

The big stove at the back of the hall is from Kavelman's Hall next door. For a while, the Farmers' Institute held meetings on the second floor of the store. A room at the back became the village library. Then Kavelman promoted the construction of a hall, which became the town centre for farmers' meetings and school meetings, for dances and any entertainment that came to town. Kavelman himself was on the library board, the cemetery board; he was a volunteer in the fire department and treasurer of the Lutheran church for 45 years.

Local people remember the 90-pound rounds of cheese in the store, and the free samples handed out to customers; the big barrel that held sugar; the fish which Kavelman imported on a Friday and cut on a slab outside the store. There were always butter and eggs and "schnitz" (dried) apples in the store, brought in by farm wives to barter for prints and wallpaper and other treasures.

Kavelman owned the store for 61 years. He had worked in it for 11 years before that. By the time he died in 1977, at the age of 95, he and his store had become a legend.

Tricia and Bill Simpson,
New Dundee, Ontario

FATHER-IN-LAW

I always thought of my father-in-law as a sentence in our Primer Reader: "The fat man stands on a hill. . . ." I always thought that's who it was. He would come out from his house on the hill to see who was going to stop at the the store. He would hear the sleigh bells. And if he liked them, he would go over and wait on them. If he didn't, he would yell at them and go over when he was ready.

But everybody liked him. He was so soft-hearted that he didn't get the outstanding money in, and finally he just had to give up.

Zaidee Williams,
Long Reach, New Brunswick

THEY LIKE 'EM THAT WAY

*I*n the 1940s, Quaker Oats was the big thing . . . 13-ounce pack, 3-pound box, 5-pound bag. Then we sold pancake flour and cornflakes, and puffed rice and puffed wheat. Puffed wheat was the biggest seller overall, but in Newfoundland we sold more puffed rice.

Newfoundland was a whole different story. I went there first in 1954 or 1955. There's some real great people there but, oh boy, they don't rush. If it's here today, it'll be here tomorrow.

I was always very concerned about the turn-over of merchandise, how fresh it was on the shelf; all our products were dated and I would check those dates. I went into a big general store, beautiful, absolutely clean, spotless, big business there, but nothing rushed about it. It was at Port au Port . . . you had to go out over a sandspit to get there. And I said, "Can I go look at your warehouse?"

"Ya, you go ahead, look around, because I'm tied up here for a while."

He had 85 cases of cornflakes stacked up neat and tidy in a pile about three high. And I looked at the date and I was absolutely horrified. They were a year-and-a-half old.

So I went back to him and said, "By the way, I'm going to ship you another 100 cases of cornflakes, and I'll give you a credit for these, we'll allow you so much for them."

"Why, is there something wrong with them?"

"Well, they've been there quite a while."

"That's O.K. They're in good shape; they're dry and clean."

"Ya, but they'll be tough."

He says, "My son, they like 'em that way down here!"

He would not let me replace those cornflakes. I hadn't seen them older any place. The flakes would be like pieces of cardboard.

Ken Gadd,
Peterborough, Ontario

CATALOGUES ON THE COUNTER

Mr. Finbow was quite a shopper. He'd go to Vancouver and go to those fire sales, and bring back oodles of goods to the Knutsford store. He kept everything. He had big tables, and there was everything from ladies' pants to horseshoes on those tables. Wasn't anything he didn't have. You could knock on his door at two o'clock in the morning and buy a 5¢ chocolate bar, and he'd have the same smile on his face as if you bought $25 of goods.

It might have been poor times, but he did well. He had a big business. In the old days, it was nothing to see 25 teams tied up there waiting for the mail. We did all our shopping there. In wintertime, we never went to Kamloops . . . maybe once in six months. Storekeepers in those days had Eaton's catalogue on the counter and Mc and Mc, which is a wholesale hardware; whatever you wanted, they'd sell it to you with a 10% discount. If Finbow didn't have it, he'd order it. In town, they wanted four times as much for a pitchfork or shovel.

Howard and Irma Humphrey,
Knutsford, British Columbia

CHRISTMAS AT MATTAGAMI HOUSE

*I*n early fall, the Indians melted away to their traplines for the winter. But they would come out again for Christmas and New Year's. Father used to make big barrels of beer from hops brought in during the fall. I made all the cookies for the Indians for New Year's. We would serve the men beer and cookies first, and the women would come in after. For New Year's, Father would make a dance, and at 12 o'clock all would go outside with their rifles to shoot the New Year in.

Jean (Miller) Leach,
Mattagami House, Ontario

THE FIRES WERE BURNING BRIGHTLY

*T*he worst snowstorm I remember was at Christmas time. I had been looking forward to going "home", and then the snow began. My husband came in, in early afternoon, and said, "We will never make it." Roads were not ploughed in those days, and our car was the little roadster with side curtains and a rumble seat.

I looked so woebegone that he finally said, "Get the boy ready and we will try . . . but we may have to turn back."

In Innisfail, Alberta in 1900, George West and Joe DeLong served customers on a polished wooden counter of superb design.

265

So we "banked" the house and store fires and asked Mr. White, a good neighbour, if he would keep fires on for us should we get storm-stayed, and set out on our 40-mile drive.

Well, we made it out . .. but didn't get back for three days. Our fires were burning brightly and nothing had frozen, thanks to Mr. White.

Marjorie Slater,
McArthur's Mills, Ontario

THE CAT IN THE BREAD BOX

Max Slemp, he was always good for a joke, but the store was atrocious . . . the cat laid in the bread box.

The Slemps were a family of 12 that came up from Oklahoma. There were nine boys in the family and they were all of the same mould. Max was stout, full-faced, with a very resonant voice. He wore glasses. He was a former school teacher. He ran a poor store. I don't know how he got the business. But everybody liked Max.

If you wanted a good clean store, you went down to Wing's Chinese grocery store. There he was decked out, blue shirt and tie, with a regular suit on; I never saw him with anything but. Cigarette holder with his cigarette in it. Behind the counter, he was very businesslike. The store was immaculate. He had a good stock in there, and there were no cats lying on the bread.

Wing was very apart from the community. He married a Russian girl when they were both getting up in years. They were a good couple. She helped him run the store. He was always smiling, very uncommunicative, but he ran an excellent store. And having married a Russian girl, the Ukrainian and Russians in the area all came to his store.

Wing's store was where the young fellows hung out during noon hour. There were punch boards. Punch boards were illegal. It was a board with 200 little holes with rolled-up pieces of paper. And you had a little metal pin that you used to punch out a rolled-up piece of paper. You paid 10¢ a punch or three for 25¢. And you unrolled it, and it gave you so many chocolate bars, or one chocolate bar or two chocolate bars or no chocolate bars. They were illegal, an under-the-counter deal. The high school boys thought they were great.

266

Nobody would squeal on Wing. If those kids had any money, they earned it; parents didn't give it to them. They stayed out of school during the fall and went on a threshing outfit, and some would end up with $50 or $100 and they just felt like millionaires.

We bought from Max because he had the personality, and that compensated. Sometimes Max's stock was out. He'd say to the customer, "Here, run and get some rolled oats at Wing's."

Max had the barbed-wire telephone which helped business, but he would have done it anyway, because it was fun. He could tell Mrs. So-and-So the latest joke, and he told some risqué ones. But he could tailor them to the individual and he got away with it.

Greta and Bob Hallett,
Fleet, Alberta

WALLPAPER

*M*ildred always sold the wallpaper. A number of women would call, asking us to send paper for a certain room, and whatever she chose for them was acceptable. On one occasion, she was away and I showed a lady the best-selling kitchen paper, but she couldn't decide on it, or on any other paper. After a long, long time, Mildred came in and took over the sale. The lady at once decided on the first paper I had showed her.

Often, the women choosing wallpaper at the dry-goods counter would ask their husbands if they liked a certain paper. The men at the grocery counter would say, "Yep, that's nice," and never turn around.

Milton Swerdfeger,
Glen Stewart, Ontario

INDEED, FRED

*M*y dad shopped at Towns' store. Dad and Billy Towns were old friends and Dad loved to joke. So this day he had decided to buy overalls. And just for fun, he said, "Billy, I would get some overalls, but the last time they didn't wear too well." (He'd bought them two years ago.)

There was a long pause, and then Billy in his soft voice said, "Indeed, Fred, and where did they seem to go first? In the knees or in the seat?" Implying that he either prayed too much or sat too much, and worked too little.

Dad laughed all the way home. He loved a joke on himself, so he was just delighted.

Muriel Fife,
Indian River, Ontario

ABSENTEE STOREKEEPER

*T*here was one storekeeper at L'Etang-du-Nord on the Magdalen Islands that I hadn't met. I had sent this chap stuff, but hadn't seen him. So I went in there about half-past ten in the morning, store wide open . . . a good big store . . . and not a soul in it. So when a fellow came in, I said, "Where is Mr. Le Blanc?"

"Oh, he's over in the school." He was the school teacher too!

"Does he come in the store here?"

"Oh yes, but not very often. But he leaves the store open and if we buy something, we write it in the book." This is how honest people were!

I went over and talked to Eli Le Blanc at the school. I said, "Do you lose anything?"

"N . . . oo," he said, "they wouldn't steal anything." He talked to the kids in French and told them he would be away a while, then came over to the store with me for an hour.

He did a fairly good business, mostly in the evenings and on weekends. But if they wanted tobacco or butter or tea during the day, they got it and marked it down on the book.

Gerald Nantes,
Magdalen Islands, Quebec

VINTAGE BOOZE

*O*ne bootlegger used to buy material from me, and I didn't really suspect what he was doing with it. But he came in one night, looking around until the others left. He had decided that

In 1980, when this picture was taken, Ruth Clark had worked over this counter for 37 years. Her dad took over the store in Millford, Ontario in 1943; she and her husband, Jack, in 1960. The clean white walls, the old shelving, the clock and the ball of string and the friendly counter are all in the best tradition of the Canadian country store.

he was dealing with me, so I should deal with him. I said, "I've no use for the stuff." I said, "O.K., I'll buy one bottle, no more. Don't ask me to buy it again." When he left, I went and hid it.

Years later, I had a chap who did me a favour and he wouldn't take any money for it. And I knew he liked to drink. I said, "I'm gonna give you something; I know nothing about it. You watch your step, take your chances!"

Next time I saw him, he said, "Where did you get it?"

"Well," I said, "that's beside the point."

He said, "I wish you could get some more."

Ben Cousins,
Rose Valley, Prince Edward Island

GOOD POP, A.J.

*L*ike my father before me, I was always supporting the Liberal Party. At election time, customers would be around looking for information, what to do, what not. And we would always have a little drink under the counter for the Liberals . . . half rum, half cider.

Cider was the big drink here before the soft drinks started. I used to get it in 10-gallon kegs from the Annapolis Valley. It was sold on the counter for 5¢ a glass. Some of those kegs you'd have on hand a while would have quite a kick in them.

There was one old gentleman, Sandy McLean . . . he was Conservative, but a very good friend . . . a man in his 80s. He would buy a bottle of pop and take some out of it, then A.J. would take him into the office and give him some good black rum as a treat. He'd come out to the other people in the store: "Well, this is good pop, A.J. This is good pop you know!" It was a little joke, just for him.

A.J. and Jessie Morrison,
North River Bridge, Nova Scotia

ALL THAT FOR A QUARTER

Mike Domm worked in the store. He was a cripple, a hunchback. Everybody knew him; everybody loved him. He could speak German, too.

Christmas Eve one year, I'd be about 12, and I had a little money, a whole quarter. I decided I was going to buy presents for the whole family. So the store was still open and Mike was there. I asked the price of everything in the store, and patiently he told me.

Finally, I think he thought he was never going to get home. So he gave me a nice linen handkerchief for Dad and something nice for everybody. I was thrilled.

Christmas morning, my family kept saying, "How in the world did you get all that for a quarter?" But Mike had given it to me, really.

Florence Maynes,
Lemberg, Saskatchewan

THEY NEVER CAME AGAIN

Mother was a very kind person and she always put herself out a little more for the Indians. One Christmas Eve, there was a family camping next to our store by the woods when the temperature was 20° Fahrenheit. She saw the little children running around the bonfire and she said to my father, "Go and see."

There were three little Indians and the mother and father. So she sent my father back. "Go and bring them in and maybe then can stay with us. I'll make up a bed on the floor."

She always made French-Canadian pork pie, *tourtière*, for Christmas. And those big doughnuts, *beignes*, rolled in icing sugar.

It started with those five people. The following year, the crowd got a little bigger and then a little bigger, so she wouldn't have them all in the house, but she would treat them. And she started making more pies and more doughnuts and more pies. And they loved black tea and sugar.

This went on for about nine years. But in 1935, Mother died of cancer. Father was still in business that next Christmas. We children who were grown up helped and we were all prepared for the Indians to come. But they never came. Mother had died on the 19th of March and they knew she was gone, and that was the end of the Indians visiting us on Christmas Eve.

Albert Emond,
Cheminis, Ontario

TIE THE HORSE TO THE OLD PINE TREE

*T*ommy Johnson was reeve and when you complained about the snowbound roads at Glen Stewart, his answer was, "It'll all be gone by July."

One winter, we had been snowed in for nearly two months. A crew of men were working with shovels in front of the big snowplough to open the road from Hainsville to Glen Stewart. Daylight was running out, and they hadn't got to our store. Mildred sent me out with the horse to say she'd feed them if they wouldn't stop until they reached the store. There was an old pine tree out there that Mildred had nicknamed Aunt Jemima . . . "Tie the horse on the right of Aunt Jemima if they will, on the left if they won't."

I tied the horse on the right of the old pine tree and stayed with a shovel to help. By eight o'clock that night, our road was open to the south, and Mildred fed the crew of 21 men.

Milton Swerdfeger,
Glen Stewart, Ontario

CONCLUSION:
NEVER SAY GOODBYE

The country store as it was in 1910 or even 1944 will never come back. It was the heartbeat of a rural lifestyle that is gone.

Stores, like any other living thing, must change. Part of the liveliness associated with their heyday, was that they were always in flux, always changing. Storekeepers read the local market as if it was the Toronto Stock Exchange, and adjusted their business accordingly.

By the 1950s the writing was on the wall. Change was occurring too fast for most local stores to adjust. The city-style supermarket and the city department store would replace the country store in most areas of Canada.

Yet such is the tenacity of the country store that 4000 of them survive. Such is the love of the way of life it served, that people in many, many places across the country still cherish and patronize their corner store. Such is the vim and vigor of many an older storekeeper that he or she won't retire. Such is the determination of certain young storekeepers that they will succeed against all odds.

This book is for them and for their customers, written in the hope that the country store will never be forgotten, and never entirely disappear.

LOCATIONS OF SOME COUNTRY STORES

ONTARIO

1. Ennismore
2. Young's Point
3. Warsaw
4. Douro
5. McCracken's Landing
6. Bethany
7. Lakehurst
8. Harwood
9. Keene
10. Bobcaygeon
11. Lindsay
12. Minden
13. Lang
14. Camborne
15. Cobourg
16. Codrington
17. Curve Lake
18. Glen Stewart
19. Morewood
20. Vernon
21. McArthur's Mills
22. Boulter
23. New Dundee
24. Ballinafad
25. Port Ryerse
26. Magwire
27. St. Augustine
28. Trafalgar
29. Mattagami House
30. Red Lake
31. Cheminis
32. Monteith
33. Porquis Junction
34. Cobalt
35. Trout Creek
36. Nipissing
37. Cold Springs
38. Millford
39. Cherry Valley
40. Rednersville
41. Heidelberg
42. Grand Bend
43. Campbellton
44. Niagara-on-the-Lake
45. Arnprior
46. Milles Roches
47. Grant's Corners

QUEBEC

48. Old Chelsea
49. Farm Point
50. Wakefield
51. St. Jovite
52. Compton
53. Grindstone
54. Grande Entrée

NEWFOUNDLAND

55. Port Au Port
56. Stephenville
57. Rocky Harbour
58. Twillingate
59. Placentia

PRINCE EDWARD ISLAND

60. Vernon River
61. Souris
62. Rose Valley
63. Crapaud

NOVA SCOTIA

64. Cape Negro
65. Port Clyde
66. Port Hood
67. Englishtown
68. North River Bridge

NEW BRUNSWICK

69. Gondola Point
70. Long Reach
71. Waterville
72. Simonds
73. Stickney
74. Glassville
75. Arthurette

NORTHWEST TERRITORIES

76. Port Burwell